Gestalt
as a Way of Life

Awareness Practices

as taught by Gestalt Therapy founders and their followers

by

Cyndy Sheldon, MSW

Illustrations by Angela Anderson

Bellingham, Washington

2012, revised 2013

Gestalt as a Way of Life: Awareness Practices

ISBN-13: 978-1484883846
ISBN-10: 1484883845
Laminated soft cover edition printed by CreateSpace Independent Publishing Platform.

Illustrations by Angela Anderson, Bellingham WA
Cover art title, "I wonder where my feet are taking me now?"

http://www.cyndysheldon.com
A spiral bound version also is offered by the author.

Book design and typography: Kathleen Weisel, weiselcreative.com, Bellingham, WA.

URLs mentioned in book were correct in September 2012.

Dedicated to
Fritz Perls, Jim Simkin,
all of my Gestalt colleagues
and
to the many students
I've worked with
over the last 50 years
who have allowed me to teach them
these timeless understandings

"Cyndy is among the pioneers of Gestalt Therapy on the West Coast. She is an engaged and talented Gestalt therapist and trainer, and an advocate of the theory and practice of Gestalt Therapy in the USA and internationally. Her wit and wisdom, her joyousness and love, continues to deepen and grow. I am grateful for all she has done to further the development of hundreds of Gestalt students."

> – **Jerry Kogan**, PhD, a licensed psychologist for 45 years, is a founder of GENI (Gestalt Educational Network International), the German Association of Gestalt Therapy (DVG) and the European Association of Counseling. He has taught in the US, Europe and Asia. He and his wife live in Frankfurt, Germany.

"Cyndy Sheldon has been a pioneer and teacher in the field of Gestalt training and therapy. As the co-founder of the original Gestalt Institute of San Francisco, she is committed to the Gestalt way of living and working. I have known her in several capacities and the one that stands out is her role as a mentor and teacher for those of us who were new in the field. She is gifted and talented!"

> – **Lucanna Grey**, MA MFT, Associate Professor of Psychology and Director of the Integral Counseling Center at the California Institute of Integral Studies (CIIS) in San Francisco.

"Cyndy Sheldon is an unusually effective and inventive Gestalt therapist. If you have the opportunity to work with her, don't miss it! I have been a friend and colleague of hers for many years and always felt her to be a superb practitioner of the Gestalt method."

> – **Dr. Lois Brien**, past member of the Cleveland Gestalt Institute and the San Francisco Gestalt Institute, and presently Dean Emeritus, School of Psychology, National University, San Diego, CA.

"I find the concepts presented by Cyndy in her workshops and now her book to be elegant and profound. The experiential exercises produced personal epiphanies that enhanced my life deeply and still help me to pay attention, in the present moment, each and every day."

> – **Dawn Gauthier**, New Zealand

Contents

INTRODUCTION

What is the Gestalt Way of Life?
What are Gestalt practices?
How did this book of practices come about?

Back in the 1960s in the San Francisco Bay Area, just as the Human Potential Movement was taking off with Fritz Perls and Gestalt therapy in the front row, everybody, it seemed, wanted to learn about themselves. It was a time to "Know Thyself", as Socrates was so famous for saying. The newly formed Gestalt Institute of San Francisco, which I co-founded in 1967 with colleagues, was booming with therapists, healers, and seekers of all kinds. They attended workshops and seminars, individual therapy and on occasion large public events held in local high schools and auditoriums to demonstrate the work of Fritz Perls and his colleagues. It was an era of experiencing the Here and Now, even before Ram Dass' book *Be Here Now* came out, an era of great excitement and growth. People bared their souls to one another. Not only did individuals attend these workshops, but couples and families came to our doorsteps. The Bay Area was alive.

SO WHAT IS GESTALT THERAPY?

Fritz and Lore Perls, born in the late 1800s, founded Gestalt Therapy and brought it to this country from Europe and South Africa in the late 1940s. Fritz was an MD, psychiatrist, and Lore was a PhD Psychologist. In Europe they had studied psychoanalysis, zen, gestalt psychology, existentialism, phenomenology, field theory, sensory awareness, and eurythmy and much more.

They chose the word Gestalt, which means "whole" or "form" to name their new therapy, attending to the whole human being, including the physical, emotional, mental and intuitive or spiritual aspects. Unlike other approaches in the early days, the focus was not on illness and dysfunction, but rather growth and excitement in human development. The Gestalt therapist invites the participant to focus on *how* he stops himself from being more alive, more contactful, more expansive, and more creative. The work is done by focusing on the minutia of experience in the now.

Gestalt therapy is best done in groups where participants can be experienced in the present by more than the therapist. This provides a rich opportunity to deal with multiple perceptions. The main goal is to invite participants to become more aware, particularly in the moment. Many practices are taught, and when participants "get stuck" or reach an impasse, the therapeutic work helps them, through awareness, experience this more clearly. The phrase "through awareness comes choice" is one used frequently by Gestalt therapists. Working through issues, unfinished business, beliefs, attitudes, is a process of discovery between the participant, the group members and the therapist. Experiential rather than intellectual understanding is key.*

THE ALIVE BAY AREA OF SAN FRANCISCO IN THE 60S

Esalen Institute in Big Sur, where Fritz resided once he moved from New York City to the West Coast, was the hub of the emerging Human Potential Movement. Other notables in the field of psychology such as Abraham Maslow, Virginia Satir, Eric Berne, and Carl Rogers were all part of this movement. Esalen was their hub, and the spokes spread out across the nation and world inspiring many to explore more about who they were. People saw themselves as growing, rather than as needing help. Instead of looking at themselves as sick, the medical model, they preferred the label "growth model".

In addition to the new therapies there were other related developments happening in the 60s: the many body therapies, such as Bio-Energetics, Reichian Therapy, Charlotte Selver's Sensory Awareness, Rolfing, massage, all of the alternative health therapies such as Acupuncture and Homeopathy, as well as psychic healing and consciousness programs. These all began to flourish alongside the more psychologically oriented approaches such as Gestalt.

There were many other related movements that flourished during the 60s and 70s: the women's movement, the Black Panthers, spiritual groups led by a number of gurus from India, Buddhism from Japan and Korea, the psychedelic movement, the anti-war movement, the student protests, the Hippies and flower children, marijuana and cheap California wine. Living in the middle of all of these creative energies and new directions was exhilarating and often overwhelming.

Eventually the Gestalt movement opened up centers all over the country and in Europe and Asia. Now you can find Institutes almost everywhere, including Russia, China, Brazil, Egypt and Israel. National and international conferences occur yearly where new ideas and ways to do the work are shared. Professional Gestalt journals exist. The academic arm of Gestalt emerged and has had a steady influence on Gestalt therapists everywhere.

But the times changed. After 20 years the excitement of Gestalt, at least on the West Coast of the USA, seemed to die down during the 80s. Some of what people thought was Gestalt therapy—such as a few of the well known techniques, slowly morphed into mainstream psychotherapy. They used these techniques to enhance their own theoretical framework and then advertised themselves as doing Gestalt therapy. Unfortunately many did not have any in-depth training and no idea of the essence of the work. Most training programs are 2-4 years in length. Luckily some Gestalt Institutes, such as those in New York, Cleveland, San Francisco and Los Angeles, kept a steady stream of students whom they trained well in Gestalt theory, practice and methodology. Today more institutes have followed suit. The graduates have done a lot of personal experiential work in both training groups and individual training therapy.

In the mid-60s, medical insurance companies began covering psychotherapy. This led to many changes in the entire field. Behavior modification, short term analytic psychotherapy, and other forms of short term therapy became the models most acceptable to these insurance companies. Gestalt and other human potential therapies took a back seat. When Gestalt therapy was first presented to the public by Fritz and Lore Perls, they presented their approach as being much quicker than traditional psychoanalysis, which was in vogue at that time. But once the insurance companies got into the act, Gestalt was no longer seen as a quick therapy. So insurance wasn't of much help since it usually covered only 5-10 sessions. Luckily there were still many who paid out of pocket in those years—however, this didn't last long, as therapists took the opportunity knowing insurance would pay, to increase their prices, thus dramatically making it hard for many to pay out of pocket.

The times became more cautious and people weren't as eager to expose themselves in public seminars and groups anymore. Then other movements evolved, such as the addiction programs, and a variety of approaches dealing with abuse. And this work was often best done in carefully protected spaces between client and therapist, rather than in workshops and seminars. Cognitive and family therapy approaches also began to flourish.

Spiritual programs were on the rise, such as Native American, Hindu, Zen, Tibetan Buddhism and Vipassana practices, to name a few. Many of those attracted to Gestalt moved towards a more spiritual approach such as Buddhism, meditation, and yoga.

During these years I was practicing and teaching Gestalt therapy in the Bay Area and abroad, watching the sociology of this movement unfold. By the 1990s, following the Loma Prieta earthquake, which devastated part of San Francisco, I felt a strong urge to leave earthquake country! I had been a guest trainer for a month at Esalen Institute in Big Sur when it hit, and I watched the earth rumble not too far from the epicenter.

THE NAVAJO INFLUENCE

My feet were literally moving me towards Arizona, to Sedona where there were interesting spiritual thinkers of the day, as well as the Navajos and Hopis nearby. I ended up working with the Navajo medicine people and elders who taught me about their way of life. For 10 years I spent time with them, running Navajo wellness conferences, a Medicine Man program, and an elder program at an Indian Health Service clinic in Winslow, Arizona.

It was during these years that I began to see some similarities in the way of life of the

Navajos and some of the Gestalt teachings. I invited co-leaders to help me put on week-long workshops addressing these two ways of life. And I discovered that many of these teachings were also similar to some Buddhist practices as well as to many of the principles put forth by Eckhart Tolle, particularly in his book *The Power of Now.*

By this time the USA was facing drought, lack of water, fear of running out of oil, and a growing number of people all over the planet were turning to their land to sustain themselves as much as possible. People wanted to stop relying on mega farms and big oil to bring products to their doorsteps from all over the world. People were simplifying their lives. My colleagues and friends in Arizona, not the best place to live off the earth, decided to follow their feet and mine led me to the Northwest where water is plentiful and the land is rich. Organic small farms are everywhere. This was in 2006. In my early 70s, I had to reinvent myself in the work world.

DEVELOPMENT OF GESTALT AS A WAY OF LIFE

More and more I realized that the Gestalt movement could be much larger than just a psychotherapeutic one. Many of us Gestalt teachers had been teaching specific practices which were part of a healing and growth process, that could be valuable to everyone. But given the fact that the founders were psychotherapists, the emphasis was put on Gestalt therapy, and the practices stayed in the background, not receiving as much attention, I felt, as they deserved. To me they are a distinct body of knowledge, separate from the therapy. They are for *everyone* to learn and enjoy, not just therapists and their clients.

So in 2007 I began offering classes for the public in both Seattle and Bellingham, Washington, titled *Gestalt as a Way of Life.* I've been teaching these ever since, and finally decided to put them in a book, so people could refer back to them frequently. To me they are like a spiritual practice, to help me center, become more aware, more alive, more creative and present with others in deep and meaningful ways.

I offer *experiments*, which are key so that you have a full body sense of these practices, and not just an intellectual understanding of them. *Experiencing fully* is one of the most important themes in Gestalt therapy. As founder Fritz Perls used to say, "every cell" in your body needs to be involved. The experiments are designed for the reader. You can adapt these or create your own for groups and classes.

I have created 7 sections with a few chapters under each. A synopsis follows.

Section A, AWARENESS, focuses on how difficult it is for some of us to be aware and our resistance to knowing ourselves well. This goes hand in hand with developing our curiosity, including paying attention to the obvious: seeing and hearing what is before us. Many of us don't see the elephant in the room. Being aware of what emerges (the emerging Gestalt) from the background, without controlling it, is another practice we encourage. All of this supports the contention that through awareness comes more choice.

Section B, GROWING UP, covers a lot of the practices about maturing rather than remaining as teenagers rebelling against the proverbial authorities, including the ones we've internalized. We look at the ways we protect ourselves from growing through our body language and the games we play to manipulate our world, our limiting beliefs, how we obfuscate our truth and hide from ourselves as well as others. Growing up turns out to be a lot more difficult than we imagined, and many of us haven't gotten very far.

Section C, GET OUT OF YOUR HEAD, is all about how we misuse and overuse our minds. We over value this aspect of ourselves, leaving out our senses and other ways of knowing by focusing on making images, theories, generalities, conclusions and minimizing the detailed phenomena we observe through our senses and intuition. Logic takes the front seat, pushing intuition and creativity to the back seat. Playing the "fitting game" and indulging in sound bites and labels is all part of this phenomenon.

Section D, AUTHENTICITY, focuses on how to be more in the here and now, and how to accept deep feelings and feelings of vulnerability. Gestalt challenges cultural shoulds, inviting you to be more in tune with your organismic self regulation, or your natural rhythm, and teaches you how to be more direct when it suits you. Being congruent is a key part of these teachings as well, similar to being in balance and harmony, ideas used by Native Americans and spiritual orientations.

Section E, THE MAGIC AND SACRED IN GESTALT, invites you to see how going fast, being in the past and future, not making contact with your full self and with others fully, being locked into planning and goal setting, can get in the way of your having magical and sacred moments in the here and now.

Section F, FINAL THOUGHTS, addresses how these practices relate to Gestalt therapy, and when it might be time to seek help. In short, it is when these practices are hard for you to do, or when you get stuck and reach an impasse.

After 50 years of teaching these practices as well as doing the therapy, I notice when meeting others with similar training and experience, we fall into a rapport of openness and understanding that is often envied by others who have not had this opportunity. Having these experiences enhances our lives, brings people together, and creates a community of people open to exploring and discovering themselves and the world around them.

I hope you find these practices fun and useful, and better yet, I hope you find like minded souls to join with you in a community of openness and sharing.

Cyndy Sheldon, MSW
Bellingham, Washington
www.cyndysheldon.com
2013

See the last section of this book for more information on Gestalt therapy.
And Mr Google will gladly help. You can also access www.gestalt.org and www.aagt.org.

Section A

AWARENESS*

1. **But I Don't Want to Become More Aware**

2. **Curiosity**

3. **Through Awareness Comes Choice**

4. **The Background and the Emerging Gestalt**

5. **Pay Attention to the Obvious**

6. **Clarity and Confusion**

*If you feel challenged doing the experiments in this section of the book, please read the chapter in **Section F: How All of These Practices Relate to Gestalt Therapy.**

Be your favorite bird looking in the window at you. What do you see?

1. BUT I DON'T WANT TO BE MORE AWARE

"If you are willing to be the Village Idiot, you probably don't need therapy." – Fritz Perls

SELF JUDGMENT AND SELF CONSCIOUSNESS

One of the most common reasons many of us do not want to know ourselves better is that we are afraid we won't like what we find out. We assume we will be more self-critical, and therefore more anxious and depressed; or we're afraid we will discover we're not as wonderful as we think we are! So the issue of a person's self-judgment and difficulty hearing constructive feedback needs attention before moving on to many of the practices in this book.

How to do this? I remind people that most of us were never taught a lot about awareness. Many of us were not raised in an environment where sharing ourselves was done. If I am teaching these practices in a class I often share my experiences and vulnerabilities. I encourage them to do the same, to get used to being open with one another. Most people will experience some self consciousness, but once the whole group gets going, this often dissipates, and they have fun with the experiments and learning.

CAUSE-EFFECT THINKING

Many people have a preconceived notion that if they become more aware of themselves and others they will *have to* make certain changes in their lives. This cause-effect thinking goes something like this:

- If I look into my sadness, I *will have to* leave my husband
- If I find out why I'm so irritable, I *will have to* quit my job
- If I read all those articles about climate change I *will have to* move
- And so on... .

Now observe this dynamic: If A, then B. A is the new thought or behavior; B is the outcome you *imagine* will happen. This neatly devised conclusion seems air tight and there seems to be no room for exploration. It is a done deal. There are many of these cause-effect beliefs we tell ourselves, and we usually aren't aware of them.

You may discover new ways of seeing, understanding and dealing with your dilemma, particularly if you share it with the parties involved, whom you've left out. You've done all the exploration in your head, even though it involves others.

In the marriage situation above, I would recommend that the wife take a risk and explore her sadness in *detail*. Then I'd encourage her to share all of this with a neutral friend or therapist. Next I'd nudge her to talk with her husband about what she has become aware of. At any of these junctures, unexpected thoughts and feelings might arise. These could lead to a very different outcome than the one she *assumed* in the beginning when she was doing all the exploring superficially, and by herself in her mind.

And maybe her assumptions are right for her, that it would be best to leave him. But even then it doesn't mean she *has to* leave now. There may be other options. And one of these options may be to table the plan to leave until later: until after their daughter graduates from high school, or after her husband's surgery. Who knows what might happen during this waiting time. The couple may have a special moment together, or see a therapist. Perhaps she has a spiritual awakening, and sees things very differently. Being open to the unexpected is also an option.

Or maybe she decides to wait *just because*. You remember that reason we used to use as kids, don't you?! It is a valid one—sometimes we *intuitively* know without the specifics being clear. So when you feel strongly that you want to do or not do something but you're not sure why, listen to your "just because."

This cause-effect dynamic is more common than you can imagine. We go inside ourselves and make zillions of assumptions about this and that, and come out of our cocoon and announce to the world our latest decision, even when it involves others.

I did this myself years ago. I was with an organization for many years and built up a lot of resentment as other members relied on me to take care of things. Over the years I expressed my concerns, but nothing changed. So after the "last straw," rather than discuss my concerns with them, I decided to leave. I did it in anger; I sent a note to everyone announcing that I was quitting. I felt relieved, self-righteous, and childish. Eventually we talked it through. And luckily my friendships with many of them remain to this day many years later. If I had been more aware of my avoiding a dialogue with them I would have requested a meeting, rather than just announcing my decision to leave.

SYNERGISTIC OUTCOMES

Often through sharing and exploring with others, new insights emerge; the energies between people affect the outcomes of their mutual concerns. Since I didn't allow for this in the case above, I missed out on what outcomes might have emerged.

This process doesn't work well unless all parties are together physically in the same room. Phone calls and skyping work less well. Email and texting don't work well at all as the parties involved are not seeing and experiencing one another fully in the moment, thus affecting the synergy.

THE UNIVERSE BEHAVES IN STRANGE AND UNEXPECTED WAYS AT TIMES and exploring the details of your concerns with *others* may lead to something you hadn't imagined. Be open to the unexpected.

EXPERIMENT

Close your eyes and ask yourself if you are reluctant to look at a specific situation in your life for fear you might have to make an unpleasant decision, like one of the ideas mentioned above. If you come up with one, be willing to look at it closely, and see if another outcome could be possible. Allow some SPACE to exist between your awareness and your imagined outcome.

2. CURIOSITY

"I wonder if I've been changed in the night? Let me think.
Was I the same when I got up this morning? I almost think I can
remember feeling a little different. But if I'm not the same, the next
question is 'Who in the world am I?' Ah, that's the great puzzle!"
– Lewis Carroll, Alice in Wonderland

I'm curious why we aren't more curious. What *blocks* us from being more curious. I know our parents went nuts when we discovered the word "why" at an early age and bombarded them with *why* questions. We were often told to keep quiet, but is that the reason we don't pursue our curiosity as adults? Did their reactions shut us up forever?

Here are what some people are not curious about that I'm aware of. I'm sure you can come up with many more.

- Why I get angry
- Why I behave in certain ways
- What we can't see or hear
- Understanding the "boxes" we're in
- Thinking and experiencing in new ways
- Getting to know ourselves better
- Getting to know those we love better
- Experiencing our anger, fear, grief and exploring their depths
- Alternative approaches to health and education
- What to do about all of the corruption and lies that seem unending
- Why the world economy is falling apart, in spite of what the media and government are telling us
- Why all the "aid" we've given to other countries hasn't helped them get above the poverty line
- Whether extraterrestrial beings exist and if some are coming to help us or hurt us

- Who controls the press; what are they leaving out and why
- Why bad things happen to good people
- And on and on and on

Curiosity is a very important quality to develop. With the Internet it is so easy to indulge our interests. However, we will find many varying views about almost everything. Many people get overwhelmed and say they don't know who to believe. They find it is too much effort to know what is reliable information and what isn't. So they quit trying. They get discouraged and then they often feel resigned. This happens in the political arena as well. If one political party appears to be distorting the truth, people throw up their hands and assume the other party is just as bad, so they avoid both. And of course this is often the intent: to turn you off of politics, particularly if you might be on the other side! Don't fall for this. Keep on being curious.

What Gestalt teachings say, is that if we become more aware, centered, and in the present we will be able to *discern* what is true and not true, and what is best for us. Most of this book is about how to develop ourselves in these ways, so read on!

EXPERIMENTS

1. **Spend a few moments with your eyes closed, a pad of paper and a pen nearby. Allow a few things to emerge that you are curious about, both themes you've explored and those you haven't.**

2. **Look at your list and get in touch with what has blocked you from exploring the unexplored themes.**

3. **Now do the opposite: allow things to emerge that you are NOT curious about. Might you be willing to risk exploring one of these now or in the near future?**

So the moral of this section is to become aware of your curiosity and to allow it to flourish!

☼

3. THROUGH AWARENESS COMES CHOICE

"Stay present and observe what is happening inside you.
Become aware not only of the emotional pain, but also of the one who
observes, the silent watcher. This is the power of the Now, the power of
your own conscious presence. Then see what happens."
– Eckhart Tolle, The Power of Now

OBSERVER

Awareness is a key principle in Gestalt learning. First we must recognize that a part of each of us is aware of the rest of us. "Who is the 'I' that is aware?" What we are referring to here is the inner observer, the witness who notices what happens—without judgment. The observer needs to be pristine. He only observes and reports. So whenever we ask you to be aware, we are inviting your observer to speak.

JUDGE

Now for the judge. As you well know, our judge is often very forceful; it takes over the witness role, or clouds it so we don't see or hear clearly. He or she sits on our throne deciding if something is good or bad, right or wrong, godly or ungodly. It happens very fast for many of us. For example, notice a behavior, such as getting a Coca Cola. Be aware if you judge yourself by saying something to yourself like "This is bad for me." Now separate the observer from the judge. The observer says "Now I'm getting a Coca Cola". The judge says "This is bad for me." These are two separate functions, but often come out of our mouths in a split second and sound like only one function. Keep them separate.

Create an example by noticing a behavior and quickly judging it positively. For example, "Right now I'm looking at my dog. She is the most special dog in the world." Separate the observation from the judgment.

So the observer just observes what is and then, right on the heels of the observation, the judge brings in a lot of its opinions. The idea here is not to stop judging, although there are many advantages in doing so. Rather the purpose is to become aware of our observing, including observing ourselves judging.

NEGATIVE JUDGMENTS

We all know it is a problem when we constantly judge ourselves "negatively". Hopefully we can distinguish between severe self criticism and constructive criticism. (See Chapter B1: *Topdog & Underdog.*)

POSITIVE JUDGMENTS

It can also become a problem if we judge ourselves positively a lot, as we may be glossing over some important feedback. There is a *should* in our culture that we must praise ourselves a lot to avoid getting depressed and to build our self esteem, which can backfire as we may avoid seeing our truth.

Many years ago a large school system instituted a program to improve self esteem by giving the children more awards and praise than usual. The hypothesis was that this would curtail some of the violence in the schools. The opposite happened; the violence increased. The kids became unrealistically sure of themselves and their abilities and became part of the "entitled" ones who insist on getting what they want when they want it.

Recently, Barbara Ehrenreich wrote a book called *Bright-Sided: How the Relentless Promotion of Positive Thinking is Undermining America*. This is full of stories about how people gloss over what is really happening to them and others in the name of "positive thinking." They avoid the truth.

EXPERIMENTS

1. *Sit quietly and observe your environment (thoughts, friends, family), without judging. Just observe and describe in detail what you see or hear. What do you become aware of when you do this without judging?*

2. *Go over the same material, and this time judge positively and negatively. What do you become aware of?*

There are no right or wrong responses, however you may discover something useful about yourself. Many people discover how hard it is to just observe and report their observations; others discover how easily they slip into judgments about themselves, using unpleasant language. One person became aware of how his negative judgments were about others, and never about himself. One lady saw how much she praised others, and not herself. This process can help you delineate different kinds of awarenesses which will likely help you in the future.

ZONES OF AWARENESS

Gestalt founder Fritz Perls created a model of three zones of awareness: the inner, the outer and the middle zones.

The Inner Zone covers what we feel emotionally, the sensations we experience in our body such as hot, cold, tense, calm, and subtle movements and vibrations. This might be an almost imperceptible ache in your shoulder or a slight twitch in one eye.

The Outer Zone covers what we see, hear, touch, taste, smell and sense outside of ourselves.

The Middle Zone includes all of our thinking processes: evaluating, judging, theorizing, concluding, amassing information and data, as well as our intuition, and imaginings.

EXPERIMENTS

1. *For a few moments, say out loud to yourself whatever you are aware of in the moment. Let each awareness emerge without controlling the process.*

2. *Check to see which zone(s) you are least aware of.*

3. *Practice paying more attention to this area in your daily life.*

For example, "I'm aware of my breathing being slow; now I'm aware of my nose tickling. Now I'm noticing the sound of my printer. Now I'm wondering when I might take a break from writing. And now I'm looking at the trees blowing in the wind outside." Then I checked to see which zones they represent. In the above example my breathing and tickling nose are in the Inner Zone; the printer sound and trees blowing are in the Outer Zone, and thinking about taking a break is the Middle Zone.

I've been asking students and clients for years which zones they are least developed in. Most said either the inner or the outer. Those in the helping professions tend to be least aware of their inner zone, and most aware in their outer zone. This makes a lot of sense, as they focus on others rather than themselves. Some of you who have worked on yourself a lot, may be quite well aware in all 3 zones.

Fritz said back in the 60s humans probably use only 10% of our capacities. It is worth expanding our awareness in all zones as much as possible, particularly the zones we attend to the least. We can *shuttle* back and forth from one zone to another, so that we don't get stuck in one or two of these areas. Years ago I became conscious of not being in touch with my inner awareness as much as the other areas. I practiced asking myself "what am I experiencing inside myself now; what are my sensations; am I feeling anything." This has helped me stay grounded and has kept me from being "in my head" too much.

Many years ago I saw a client in the neat and tidy office I was renting in San Francisco. The next week part of this office had been torn up for remodeling. This client didn't notice a thing. He was very aware of all his inner experiences and his thinking and judging, but he had no awareness of what was around him in his environment. This was representative of his problem in life: he was stuck and couldn't relate to his world or to others very well. By attending to others in his environment (Outer Zone) he experienced a lot of fear of others, which eventually led to his dealing with this issue, becoming more open to connecting with others and being less alone.

A number of clients, well developed in their outer zone, pay close attention to everyone and everything around them. But they have no sense of their inner sensations or world. In an extreme case they are incapable of knowing if something that happens makes them feel uncomfortable or upset or angry or sad. When invited to get in touch with their inner self, some have said "I am afraid. There might not be anything there. I don't know who I am. Maybe I'll find out I'm a bad person", etc. Working with these people to find an inner core, can be most exciting and profound for them. They can then let go of their incessant need to hurry and keep focused on the Outer or Middle Zones to avoid experiencing themselves deep inside.

In Gestalt we don't encourage people to stop doing a behavior, but rather to do new behaviors more often. So if you are undeveloped in one of the zones of awareness, consciously pay more attention to it. Do it playfully and often. Gradually you will become more balanced in your awareness.

4. THE BACKGROUND AND THE EMERGING GESTALT

Out of the caterpillar's cocoon emerges a butterfly.

Being aware of the background and the context of everything is most important in our understanding of what is going on. The foreground does not exist without the background. The butterfly does not exist without the caterpillar and the cocoon. The background includes the location, culture and times that we're living in as well as the cultural and personal histories of the players. This is what some refer to as getting in touch with the "big picture". There of course is a bigger picture, if we want to go out into the cosmos… and beyond.

It is out of the background that something emerges into the foreground and attracts our attention, without our choosing it. When we hear a child cry, we first attend to her in the foreground and then we become aware of the background and the context to understand what happened to her. We are making this context the foreground when we attend to it.

Other times we may purposely chose something to focus on bringing it into the foreground. For example, late at night, I may pick up a book I am reading, letting everything else I've been doing recede into the background. Again, we hopefully will pay attention to the background from which it came.

Some don't attend to the background. They miss the context. And many people assume they are operating from the same story. For example, someone might call on the phone and begin a long conversation, assuming the listener is free to listen for some time. They might not ask if the person is free to talk at that moment, or if they are busy. I've worked with many couples around this issue, inviting the talkative one to check in with her partner to see if he has time to listen to her. Give him a lead line or a paragraph heading and ask if he is available. This way she is honoring him and what he has been involved with prior to her talking to him. She might have to learn to be sensitive to the context from which he is emerging at that moment.

The background also includes more than what is obvious in the moment. The phrase "cultural sensitivity" refers to our need to understand where people are coming from. The history of Native Americans, Asian Americans, Euro Americans and African Americans we know affects who they are in the moment. Are we aware of their history? We may make a lot of *assumptions* here that might be wrong. Yet attending to the background is well worth the endeavor particularly when we can check out our assumptions.

The Introduction to this book is about my background involvement with Gestalt and the background of what was happening when Fritz Perls brought Gestalt Therapy to the USA and the West Coast. Fritz' history of being Jewish in Berlin when Hitler arrived in the 1930s informs us of some of the influences that affected Fritz and his wife, Lore, and the development of Gestalt Therapy. By focusing on this, I've brought this information into the foreground.

The background and foreground obviously have a relationship with one another. Depending on where your attention is, the foreground and background may change from moment to moment and may change places. There often is a constant ebb and flow. Seeing from different vantage points can always be informative and thus increase your awareness.

EXPERIMENTS

1. *Squint your eyes to make the scene in front of you blur. Now slowly allow something to come forth from the background scene to attract your attention. It might be a flower, a person walking down the street, a garbage can. Notice how things from the background attract your attention. Experiment with choosing what emerges and letting it happen naturally. For example as kids in the car we used to see how many red lights we'd see on a long trip, or how many birds, etc.*

2. *Imagine you are an extraterrestrial (ET) and you zoom in slowly coming from outer space to look into your life on earth. Have fun with this using Google Earth to get a sense of the vastness in space (background) as you move slowly into your real earth life seeing your country, state, countryside, community, and home. What do you experience as the ET?*

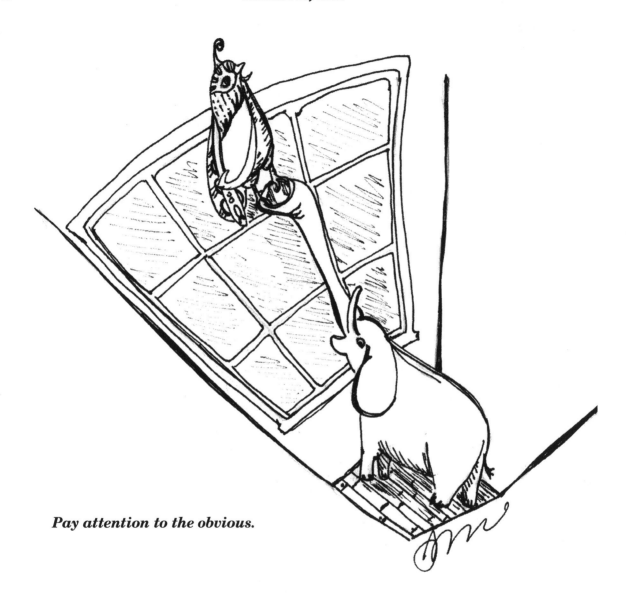

Pay attention to the obvious.

5. PAY ATTENTION TO THE OBVIOUS

"A neurotic is someone who is not aware of the obvious." – Fritz Perls

Fritz Perls used the phrase "pay attention to the obvious" a lot. He applied it to himself back in the 30s in Germany. His concern about what was going on politically was scoffed at by his colleagues and when he decided to leave Berlin in 1933 these same colleagues accused him of being paranoid. Fritz and Lore Perls escaped from Hitler and many of their colleagues did not. (He later coined the phrase "Healthy Paranoia")

In some ways this command "pay attention to the obvious" is like telling people to notice the elephant in the room. Why does no one see it? It is so obvious. And huge. Yet we often don't. We are too busy distracting ourselves with a zillion things. Here are some of the ways we miss the obvious.

- We don't want to know what is really going on. For example many partners of sexual abuse perpetrators don't know what their partner is doing, often in their home
- Thinking, thinking and more thinking, so much so that we aren't aware of what is going on in our environment or inside ourselves
- Only looking down, up and around instead of directly at someone. Or only looking directly at someone and not around
- Looking only inside oneself or only outside oneself
- Enjoying our addictions
- Being stuck in rigid belief systems: as "my partner would never put on a surprise birthday party for me" or "our government would never let that happen to us"
- Being distracted by our self consciousness, and constantly worrying if we are OK or not OK
- Seeing only the big picture and missing the important small details
- Seeing only the small details and missing the big picture

Every cell in our body is receptive to knowing, not just our minds. So it is important to pay attention to what *all of us* is experiencing in all three awareness zones.

EXPERIMENT

1. *Imagine you are an Eagle (or a favorite bird of yours). You are able to hear, see, smell and know everything going on as you look down on your life as a human. From the vantage point of one of these magnificent birds what obvious things do you see as you look in the window at yourself? Be very specific. Write things down.*

2. *Since we all have blind spots, ask a friend if they are aware of something obvious in our lives that we aren't noticing. Perhaps we don't take in fully how our partner treats us at times, or how we tense up every time our boss enters the room, or if we miss fully experiencing the loving hug from our child.*

6. CONFUSION & CLARITY

"Now is the time for confusion." – I Ching

On a related theme, many think something is wrong with them if they are confused and not clear all the time. Well, please be easy on yourself. We normally go through a state of confusion on the way to getting clear. It is an important stage in clarifying the emerging gestalt.

There is little tolerance in our society for confusion. Many are embarrassed if they aren't clear. They may go so far as to make up "clarifications" to satisfy themselves and others rather than acknowledge they aren't clear.

Often I encourage people to pay attention to their inner experience, which may be just sensations, without any clarity as to the meaning of the sensations. I invite them to be satisfied with knowing this much, and saying something like: "Something doesn't feel right. I'm not sure exactly what it is. I'm not clear now, and I will just have to accept that. I may never come up with a clear reason. I trust my sense that it doesn't feel right. "

Years ago I threw the coins for the I Ching (Chinese Book of Changes), and I was guided to a section in the book that stated "Now is the time for confusion. Now is not the time for action." I was delighted to see that it honored the state of being confused. May you do the same. Allow it to be there; increase your awareness and when it is time, clarity may emerge. And it may not!

Do stay away from using "I'm confused" or "I don't know" as excuses, a game many young ones play to protect themselves from critical parents and teachers.

EXPERIMENT
Imagine telling a friend or loved one that you are confused. And let them know that you don't have a "should" that you must be clear all the time. Notice the reaction you get.

Section B

GROWING UP*

1. **Topdog/Underdog: Our Internal Authoritarian Conflict**

2. **Telling Ourselves the Truth**

3. **Don't Push the River; It Flows by Itself**

4. **How We Protect Ourselves with Postures and Gestures**

5. **How We Protect Ourselves with the Games We Play**

6. **How our Beliefs Limit Us**

7. **The Holes in our Personality**

8. **Responsibility**

*If you feel challenged doing the experiments in this section of the book, please read the chapter in **Section F: How All of These Practices Relate to Gestalt Therapy.**

1. TOPDOG & UNDERDOG:
OUR INTERNAL AUTHORITARIAN CONFLICT

"Our dependency makes slaves out of us, especially if this dependency is about our self esteem. If you need encouragement, praise, pats on the back from everybody, then you make everybody your judge." – Fritz Perls

When we were all children our parents or caregivers needed to run the show for many years. Gradually, hopefully, they handed the reigns over to us, making us equals to them. But often this shift did not happen on an internal level, so we now continue the parent/child dynamic inside ourselves, messing up our lives and relationships. If this dependent child matures, he no longer needs a judge, externally or internally. He can stand on his own two feet and relate to others in meaningful ways.

In the early 20th Century well known philosopher Martin Buber coined the phrase "I and Thou", (which also became a book title of his), to describe the mature egalitarian relationship. Having grown up in an authoritarian society Fritz was subject to others telling him what to do—from the German government, to his parents, to his psychoanalysts who told him why he behaved the way he did, and lastly to the inner authoritarian voice inside himself. The latter he named his Topdog, and what followed naturally was his awareness of his Underdog.

Gestalt therapy invites us to work through our topdog underdog conflicts and come to an I-Thou relationship within ourselves, where both aspects listen and observe the other fully in the present. Much of Gestalt teachings are about how to make contact in this way.

Fritz Perls worked with participants in his workshops extensively with these warring parts. He'd have each part take a different chair, and dialogue back and forth. The topdog is usually critical, judgmental, authoritarian, parent-like.

Often the underdog is less well known to us, as he can be subtle and secretive, so we may focus more on the topdog who is more obvious and is usually constantly evaluating us. The underdog can be compliant, seemingly agreeing with the topdog, or saying yes, and then doing the opposite. Or it can be subtle (clenching our jaws) and secretive, or obviously defiant and rebellious. Some people aren't aware of having a rebellious part, that is until they begin to explore it, and if there is any spark of life in a lifeless compliant underdog, this is good news! Look for her!

Inherent in this dynamic, is the lack of egalitarian treatment of ourselves toward ourselves and toward one another. No one likes to be told what to do even inside our own heads!

EXPERIMENT
Have a dialogue between your topdog and underdog about a "should" dear to your heart. Many feel they "should" spend more time with their partner or children, work harder, get another degree, relax more, etc. Pick your favorite. If you don't think your underdog is anything other than compliant, look again. How does it feel to be told what to do?

HIERARCHY AND HOW THIS THEME PLAYS OUT IN THE WORLD
AND AMONG GESTALT INSTITUTES AND STAFF

Fritz saw this authoritarian dynamic not only within each of us, but in the organizational and political realms as well. In his early life he became politically active in Berlin against the authoritarian government, which Hitler was leading at the time. Fritz and his wife Lore, sensed the danger awaiting them if they stayed in Germany. They left Berlin in 1933.

So, he was staunchly against "hierarchy". He felt strongly that there should *not* be a Gestalt hierarchy, where some at the "top" could tell those at the bottom who was ok and who wasn't, as was and maybe still is the case in a number of psychotherapy organizations of other persuasions. So there is no such international or national Gestalt organization based on a hierarchical structure. The Gestalt Institute of San Francisco, which I co-founded and taught at for over 20 years, was a co-op, with 10 faculty members equal in power. This system had its drawbacks, but it basically followed the egalitarian principles so strongly adhered to by the Gestalt founders.

LABELING AS A FORM OF HEIRARCHY AND CONTROL

Martin Buber's I and Thou approach is taught in many different ways in the work. Gestalt teachers teach trainees to see one another without labels, to hear one another clearly, and to honor the other as equals. (See Chapter C5: *The Problems of Labeling.*)

Fritz was adamant that "the doctor does NOT know best". He said many times that the client is capable of knowing himself more than anyone else, and the therapist is there to guide the client through experiments with new ways of being and experiencing his world. Jim Simkin, Fritz' frequent co-leader on the West Coast, said that he sees himself as a "mid-wife" assisting the birth of the new you.

GESTALT THERAPIST BEING AUTHENTIC

Also as part of the I and Thou principle, Gestalt therapists and teachers are encouraged to be real and authentic in the relationship with their clients and students, a big departure from main stream psychotherapy principles. This does not mean that the therapist uses the client, who is paying him, to talk about his life and problems as one would with a friend, perhaps. But rather, he is present in the moment with the client, and he responds like any human might respond, which is often revealing about who he is. In this way the client is encouraged to see and hear him, making genuine contact, rather than making contact with his *image* of the therapist, which is often inflated.

If you have a topdog who is still very critical of you, you are still caught in the inner authoritarian dynamic of inner parent criticizing inner child, it probably means that you haven't learned how to treat yourself as an equal yet. Once your internal dynamic shifts, you can move more easily into an egalitarian relationship with others and your world. You will stop letting others run your life, and you will stop trying to run the lives of others!

2. TELLING OURSELVES THE TRUTH

"Change occurs when one becomes what he is, not when he tries to become what he is not." – Arnold Beisser, MD

OUR TRUTH IN THE MOMENT

A well-known Los Angeles Gestalt therapist, Arnold Beisser, MD, wrote the above comment about his theory called the Paradoxical Theory of Change. (Google has his article in full.)

If we can acknowledge what is true in the moment, our mind-body-spirit becomes aligned. We become congruent as long as we accept what is. We don't have to like what is true in the moment. We only have to acknowledge it. Then we can move on. If we don't acknowledge what is true in the moment, we remain stuck in a state of tension or anxiety between *what is* and *what we want*. And in this state we can't move on. We need to acknowledge the truth in the moment first. Below is a brief session with a workshop participant to illustrate this idea.

Gestalt Session with M

Missy, new to Gestalt, volunteered. She had expectations that she *should* get in touch with something important inside of herself.

C: What are you aware of?

M: I feel a sensation of fluttering in my chest, sort of like butterflies.

C: Can you give the butterflies a voice?

M: (as the butterflies) I'm afraid. I'm afraid of not finding anything inside of me. I feel disconnected from myself.

C: You are acknowledging what is true for you in the moment, which we have been discussing. Can you now say these same sentences to each of us as you make eye contact with us.

M: (She repeats the sentences as requested.) The butterflies have diminished! I feel more connected with myself now.

C: By owning what is true in the moment you came back to yourself. You are no longer split between what you thought you should be and who you are in the moment.

As long as there is a conflict between what is and what we want, we are stuck. In the situation above, Missy *imagined* she had nothing inside herself. She became anxious and no movement could occur. Once she acknowledged and accepted her truth in the moment, she became aligned and balanced; her anxiety dissipated. Then she became relaxed and open to something new emerging. She later discovered many aspects of her *inside* self.

WANTING

Every time we use the word "want" it is about the future, even if it is only a minute from now. The state of wanting is one that TV ads encourage, that our educational and professional cultures encourage—always "striving" for something more in the future. It is no wonder being in the now is so difficult for us. We are hard wired to be in the state of wanting, and to constantly ask ourselves what we want. Our culture demands it, and unfortunately many therapists and counselors demand it as well.

NEEDING

An interesting twist on the above occurred many years ago, when I was 20. I had a summer job working in a Dime Store, for those of you who can remember back then. The community I was in was an upper middle class one, so most who entered the store had plenty of dimes to spend. One day a mother and her 5 year old son came in. The son started dragging his mother around screaming "Mommy, Mommy, what do I need! What do I need!" He was obviously taught to get in touch with his needs. Were needs ok but not wants? At any rate he became hysterical when he couldn't get his mother to tell him what he needed! He was in the future, not in the present and he was off balance and upset. I recall feeling sorry for this young boy and wondered what on earth his parents were trying to achieve by teaching this idea to him.

It is bad enough if we get hysterical about not getting what we need, but to not even know what we need adds another stress to our existence! Years later I met Lillie Tomlin and told her this story. She asked if she could use it in one of her skits, which I said yes to, of course. I never found out if she did, but she was certainly affected by it, as was I.

WE 'SHOULD' BE BETTER THAN WE ARE

So much emphasis in our culture is on what we aren't: smart enough, strong enough, pretty or handsome enough, rich enough, and the list goes on and on. So we set *goals;* we make New Year's Resolutions; we set up many *shoulds* for ourselves to obey. And if we don't obey these *shoulds* we more than likely become very *critical* of ourselves. (See Chapter B1: *Topdog & Underdog.*) And often this approach doesn't work well with us. Why not? Because most of us don't like being told what to do, by ourselves or anyone else! Other avenues may emerge that are more important if we are open to listening to ourselves without judging and creating this dysfunctional dynamic of the topdog and underdog.

WHAT WE THINK WE WANT MAY NOT BE IN OUR BEST INTEREST

This process of acknowledging our truth in the moment may not lead to what we think we want, but it may lead to what we need. As the Rolling Stones sang in the 70s, "You can't always get what you want, ...but you just might get what you need."

Rather than asking what we want, a Gestalt therapist will more likely ask "What are you aware of right now; what are you experiencing now?" These are good questions to ask ourselves as they invite us to tune into our inner self *right now.* What we are in touch with inside may not be what we think we want. Acknowledge this, too. Don't run away from these awareness's. Accept them and see what happens. *Be open to the unexpected.*

When I was in Arizona, I had a vision of a glass dome covering Flagstaff with an open window to the East. My first response was "Oh, No, I don't *want* to live in Winslow", the town east of Flagstaff. I didn't fight the vision; I accepted that I had it although I was very unhappy about what I assumed it meant. And then things unfolded for me. I moved to Flagstaff after finding a job in Winslow at the Indian Health Service 3 days a week, which I loved. If I hadn't acknowledged my vision, I might never have sought a job with the Navajo people. That would have been a big loss for me.

NAVAJO TRUTH TELLING SIMILAR TO GESTALT'S

I learned many things from the Navajos I knew, such as their dedication to speaking specifically, directly and truthfully, values that are true in Gestalt as well. I found the following poem written in 1890 by a Navajo man, which speaks of the importance of telling the truth.

I am humbled before the earth
I am humbled before the sky
I am humbled before the dawn
I am humbled before the evening twilight
I am humbled before the blue sky
I am humbled before the darkness
I am humbled before the sun
I am humbled before that standing within me
which speaks with me
Some of these things are always looking at me
I am never out of sight
Therefore I must tell the truth
That is why I always tell the truth
I hold my word tight to my breast.
– Tom Torlino, Navajo, c. 1890

EXPERIMENTS

1. *This next experiment was one of Fritz' favorites. Begin some sentences with "The truth is in this moment I am..." This sentence is something to say to yourself often, as it brings your attention back to yourself, to what is going on inside of you in the moment. For example: "The truth is at this moment my shoulders are tense from sitting too long at the computer. I have been in my mind and unaware of my physical body. By saying this sentence now, I avoid the pain I would have felt if I had stayed out of touch with my body much longer. Thank you, Fritz, for teaching me this sentence." Practice this a lot!*

2. *It is said that we are leaving the Piscean Age, the age of secrets, and moving into the Aquarian Age, the age of revealing secrets. Many of us thought this applied only to large groups such as priests, governments and corporations, which it does. But to us personally? What secret have you not acknowledged to yourself? Be aware of how you feel after doing so. For example as a teenage girl, I pulled away from my mother. This was hard for me to acknowledge at first. Now it is easier.*

3. *If you feel shame or guilt with the last exercise, acknowledge that truth, too. Can you accept the truth about yourself? Say them over and over. We are all human, and you don't have to like your truths, only accept them. See what effect that has on you. Maybe you will drop some of your perfectionist expectations?*

3. HOW WE PROTECT OURSELVES WITH POSTURES, GESTURES, AND VOICE

"Give your clenched fist a voice." – Fritz Perls

In order to survive as kids we had to find whatever ways we could to protect our fragile egos from those around us, whether they were overbearing, ignoring, or mean and cruel, or even seriously abusive. We couldn't confront the adults or walk away without serious repercussions, so we had to find other ways to protect ourselves. Often without realizing it, we did strange things to our bodies by twisting, tilting, tightening our faces, bodies, voices and eyes. For many of us, these physical movements became chronic patterns which we may use to this day whether we need to protect ourselves or not. Some of them are just bad habits, and stopping them can be relatively easy. We also developed many social games, which Eric Berne so brilliantly noticed and wrote about in his book *Games People Play*. These games, will be discussed in the next chapter.

While growing up, many advised us not to be open, clear and direct. Never show your anger. Never tell or show your enemy you are afraid of him, they would say. So we became more subtle and devious, so much so that we often fooled ourselves as well as others. We became split off from our feelings of hurt, fear, vulnerability and anger. These feelings often became locked up in our bodies, hidden from us and others. Our subtle postures and gestures could deflect any blow coming our way, at least up to a point.

For example, years ago while teaching in Germany I noticed a trainee staring at me during our work together. Hans' eyes were locked and blocked so that no feeling could come through them as he described some painful experiences in his life. When I brought his staring to his attention he told me he was beaten if he didn't look at his parents when they were talking to him. So we worked on this for awhile; I encouraged him to let his eyes go where they wanted to go. He learned to look away when he felt like it. And come back when it felt right again. Back and forth in his own rhythm until his eyes became less rigid and locked. Feeling slowly came back to him, and he rejoiced when he finally was able to cry again.

There are thousands of examples of this. Here are a few that stand out for me over the many years I've been doing Gestalt therapy.

Sally was a young woman who would string her words together without pausing at the end of each sentence. She just kept going on and on, and then she would change the subject without pausing, and wonder out loud how she was doing, but still never paused or put a period at the end of any of her sentences. Needless to say, others became very frustrated as she made it difficult for others to get a word in edgewise. And there was rarely any dialogue. When we explored this behavior, she became aware that if she paused her parents might criticize her or her siblings might make fun of her. So pausing was dangerous for her. Gradually after experimenting with pausing, she became more comfortable dialoging and discovered people didn't pull away from her so much. She had not realized why they did so until she did this work.

Another example is Marion, a woman who tilted her head to the side each time she asked for something. Some people experienced this behavior as cute, coy and charming and couldn't resist giving her what she wanted. Others felt manipulated by her and cut her out of their lives. She was distressed and wondered why, and again, once she became aware of trying to charm people by tilting her head she experimented with stopping it and asking directly for what she wanted. This was scary for her, but eventually she learned to tolerate people saying "no" on occasion.

And then there was Harriet, a person who spoke so quietly the listener had to move closer to hear what she was saying. Harriet became aware that she was afraid of saying something "wrong" and being ridiculed. She experimented with speaking louder, and taking responsibility for what she said. Eventually she learned to tolerate others disagreeing with her.

And then there was Peter who always looked down or away, and rarely if ever made eye contact. Eventually when he risked looking at me, he got in touch with some shame about an early event in his life. He continued to make eye contact with others and with the support he received, it became easier for him to be more present with himself and the others in the group.

In Gestalt we explore the nonverbal ways we experience our worlds and what these postures and gestures are saying. As you can see from the above example, these can be very powerful and reactions to changing these postures must be taken seriously.

Here are a few examples of things to watch for when in contact with someone else.

- Holding our breath
- Looking away, above someone, or to the side
- Looking through someone, but not being there
- Smiling or laughing a lot
- Clenching our jaws
- Locking our chests, tightening our abdomen or anus
- Looking down at someone, while head is tilted back
- Looking up at someone, though our heads are down
- Tilting our heads to the right or left
- Pushing our eyebrows together, or lifting them up
- Squinting
- Over-animated facial expressions
- Under-animated facial expressions
- Standing sideways so we can walk off at any moment

Many of these protections are physically bad for our bodies and keep us out of balance which means our energies don't flow openly and fully. A Gestalt therapist will invite you to become aware of these habits, give them a voice and see what these gestures are trying to say. For example: my tight jaw might be saying "I'm mad" or "I'm scared." There are no set responses. Generalizations about the meaning of certain postures should be avoided. Most important is for you to find out what *your* body is saying.

When you choose to stop a gesture, be kind to yourself if you can't make it go away quickly. It is ingrained in your being. Just become aware and change it in the moment again and again. Eventually stopping it will become more automatic.

EXPERIMENTS

1. *Become aware of your postures and gestures: imagine they can speak to you in words. Give them a voice, and see what they are saying to you. For example, be your headache talking to you. Then respond and continue the dialogue. You can do this in writing or by setting up a couple of chairs and shuttling back and forth as you play both parts.*

2. *Experiment with stopping the gesture, which may be harming you (holding your breath when you meet someone, for example). If you don't need to protect yourself anymore, fine. But if you do, find a healthier response, such as excusing yourself or stepping back to give yourself more breathing room.*

3. *It is often said that 90% of what couples say to one another is non-verbal. Watch a sitcom on TV with the sound off, paying attention to body language and facial expressions. You will learn a lot about non-verbal communication!*

The smallest postural change such as the tilt of your head or the slight change in your breathing, may seem insignificant, but in the grand scheme of things, being aware of it might be one of the most helpful awarenesses in your life!

4. HOW WE PROTECT OURSELVES WITH THE GAMES WE PLAY

"We are spoiled and we don't want to go through the hell gates of suffering: we stay immature; we go on manipulating the world rather than suffer the pains of growing up." – Fritz Perls, 1969

Eric Berne, MD, founder of Transactional Analysis and author of *Games People Play* was in San Francisco teaching at the same time that Gestalt founder Fritz Perls was leading training workshops in Gestalt therapy. The two met on numerous occasions, and Eric attended Fritz' 75th birthday bash at San Francisco's Miyako Hotel, the year before Fritz died. Virginia Satir, MSW, was one of the first to put family therapy on the map. She also focused on the roles and games we each developed in our family of origin to get what we wanted. Fritz and Virginia connected at Esalen Institute in Big Sur during the 60s and learned from one another.

From Fritz' point of view we all develop ways to get what we want in the world and to protect ourselves. Little children become manipulative when they don't have enough power in a family or are too young to ask for what they want in an open and direct manner. And if the family is very toxic or abusive, children will develop roles to protect themselves as much as possible. We all know examples of manipulation: bullying, being coy and cute, looking like a victim, etc. Examples of protective roles might be: a child who withdraws as a way of protecting himself in a volatile family. Another is a child who might rebel and run away from home. Whether a child is being manipulative or protective the games they develop often carry on into adulthood when they may not need to behave in such ways.

If you ask directly for what you want, you risk being told "no". Learning to risk this is important, as it teaches us not to attempt to control others. But if I can manipulate you, I've learned a way to influence or control you, which may work for only a short while. Much of Gestalt work is about growing up and dealing with this issue: moving from immaturity to maturity, where we stop manipulating our environment and stand on our own two feet. (See Fritz' quote above.)

Children are often taught roles. Boys are often taught to be strong and tough, ignoring their vulnerabilities. Girls are often taught to be seductive, "to get a man." If these games are successful, they are hard to give up. However, they aren't successful at becoming a whole complex mature human being who treats themself and others as equals.

Playing games to manipulate and protect render us inauthentic and superficial. Since they involve controlling others, the others may not comply after a while, which can lead to dissatisfaction and loneliness and eventually more serious states such as depression. And don't forget that playing games to control others is a form of authoritarian control.

EXPERIMENT
Write down the role or roles that you are aware of playing with your friends and family growing up. You may have played a different role in school than at home. Are you still playing these games as an adult? Get to know yourself more fully, as the more you know, the more options you have to risk being less manipulative and more open, direct and mature.

This does not mean that we have to give up some delightful parts of ourselves fully! A good friend of mine, who died at the age of 96, said on his death bed to his wife: "I just can't be charming anymore." It took too much effort at this stage of his life. And what a charmer he was, a part of him we all delighted in. He was also an excellent psychotherapist and a person dedicated to working on himself until the very end.

Don't push the river; it flows by itself.

5. DON'T PUSH THE RIVER; IT FLOWS BY ITSELF*

> *"Some people have the idea that we create our own reality, but this notion is disrespectful to the universe. It doesn't honor the complexity of existence. We are neither making life happen, nor is life simply forcing us to do things. There is an exchange, an interaction."*
> *– Leslie Grey, The Good Red Road*

Our culture teaches us we can have whatever we want in life. And if we don't create it, something is wrong with us. So we work hard at creating our reality, and often we push and pull to make it happen. This process is taught to us everywhere: parents, school and even spiritual quests. To do so assumes we have total control over our lives; that we can push and pull the river of our lives any way we please. We learn many ways to manipulate our world, or to be more polite "to create strategies to get what we want." And the *bad* things that happen to us we created as well: marriages, illnesses, and failures, probably because we didn't use the right strategies.

If my teenager isn't turning out to fulfill my expectations of becoming an A student, then I might push and pull him, berate and intimidate him, until he hopefully does what I want. I assume control of how he turns out. Allowing him to be who he is, might be something I've never considered.

Or on a more personal level, maybe I want to be seen as a very nice person. So I support and praise others, and never (or almost never) get upset with them or judge them. I hide or ignore my inner experience, my tensions and exhaustion keeping up this facade of 'niceness'. I created my own reality, but...

In both of these cases I have *shoulds* for myself and my son. I push and pull and attempt to control both of us, and often this only leads to rebellion on his part. He walks away from me. I begin to see how tense my body is all the time, being nice when I don't feel like it. (See chapters B1: *Topdog & Underdog*. D6: *Congruence*.) To keep pushing and pulling is like trying to change the course of a river. Something is very wrong with this philosophy which is so prevalent in our society. Again, pushing and pulling is a form of authoritarian control.

WHAT ALTERNATIVES ARE THERE?

Finding out what my son wants might be a good idea. When a Navajo child is born, the family begins to watch this unique child very carefully to see what emerges as this child's special ability and offering. They don't burden their children with expectations like our dominant culture seems to do.

And maybe I ought to ask myself the same question? What would make me less tense and more satisfied. Do I *want* to be nice all the time? Often we set unrealistic and inauthentic goals for ourselves which leads to frustration, exhaustion, inauthentic behavior, loss of connection with loved ones, and on and on. And then we strategize and try to make it happen by whatever means are available, including pushing, pulling, and manipulating.

ALLOWING THE EMERGING GESTALT

To do this we invite our intuition and unconscious to take center stage. We learn to be aware of the *emerging Gestalt*. Our task is to *allow* (an important process in Gestalt) whatever wants to emerge, without controlling or changing it. This involves being in the present, the here and now, watching for what emerges next in our awareness.

Sometimes this can be frightening as we may not want to see what emerges. Once a client was about to get married. His fiancé fit all of his logical requirements: she had a good job, was young and attractive; she laughed at his jokes and praised him a lot. But he kept having nightmares that he shouldn't marry her. Finally he went into therapy to discover what was going on with him. Slowly and painfully he became more aware of himself and of her in minute detail. He hadn't been paying attention to the nuances of their relationship and to his responses to her. He had been "putting up" with a lot of things that upset him, discounting his responses as being negligible. He hadn't been present in the moment a lot of the time. He ignored the *emerging* clues until his dreams woke him up.

Fritz Perls honored emerging awareness and felt it would get us closer to the truth of who we are more than anything else. And he taught us how to recognize when our clever minds were either trying to control us or were reacting to the control. Both behaviors ignore and distract us from our deeper emerging self. Don't push the river. It flows by itself.

Most of our education and training in the USA emphasizes our left brain activity, our logical and reasonable side. It does not give equal attention to our right brain activity, our intuitive, creative side. In Gestalt many of the experiments emphasize the right brain, as it has many unexpected surprises for us.

EXPERIMENT

1. *Notice an example in your life where you have tried to influence or control someone else rather than allow them to be who they are. Offering a suggestion to that person can be helpful, but trying to control, or push their river usually doesn't work! Examples could be your wanting a spouse, child, a sibling to change. If they experience you in anyway as a topdog controller, they will probably rebel, secretively or out front, and reveal their underdog.*

2. *Do the same with yourself. Recall an example of trying to control yourself (topdog) and see what your underdog does in response. Can you push your own river?*

3. *Role-play being a river by describing yourself as this river. Start some sentences with "I am a river; I am..." Do this until you want to stop. Then continue a little longer. Notice all the many aspects you've attributed to your river.*

4. *Say the same sentences you said about the river about yourself. See if any of them fit you. Did you learn anything more about yourself doing this? Maybe you are a lot more dynamic and intricate than you thought?*

When I role played being a river, I kept saying things like "the shore affects me as the river, and I as the river affect the shore" or "sometimes a storm will cause me, the river, to flow fast, and sometimes constant summer sun will quiet me, as the river, to almost a standstill." As Leslie Grey notes in the quote at the beginning of this chapter, "We are neither making life happen nor is life simply forcing us to do things. There is an exchange, an interaction."

*Barry Stevens, one of Fritz Perls' early Gestalt students on the West Coast took this phrase, "Don't push the river; it flows by itself.", presumably coined by Fritz Perls, and used it as the title for her well known Gestalt book published in 1970.

6. HOW OUR BELIEFS LIMIT OUR ALIVENESS

"Don't be trapped by dogma—which is living with the results of other people's thinking. Don't let the noise of others' opinions drown out your own inner voice. And most important, have the courage to follow your heart and intuition." – Steve Jobs, Apple CEO

ALIVENESS

When a baby is happy, his whole body expresses movement and excitement; when he is sad, his whole body expresses grief; when he is mad his whole body expresses rage. The notion here isn't that we "should" express ourselves like a baby whenever we feel deeply about something, but rather that we are *able* to do so.

Experiencing fully, experiencing our aliveness are definitely values Fritz Perls adhered to in developing Gestalt therapy. He encouraged us to experience with all the cells in our body. He invited us to develop the ability again to feel all of our feelings and to be able to express them, as a healthy baby would. As adults many of us have trained ourselves not to experience certain feelings, which of course, affects us. We have chronically restricted our bodies through developing gestures and postures so that we can't cry or raise our voices fully or laugh with our whole being. (See Chapter B3: *How We Protect Ourselves with our Postures, Gestures, and Voice.*)

Wilhelm Reich, who developed Reichian therapy, was Fritz' training analyst in Europe just before WWII. He encouraged people to feel fully, and provided a breathing therapy to elicit unexpressed emotions about experiences and events in the past that were locked into body tissues. Although Fritz didn't use these methods, he valued Reich's work, particularly in his understanding body armoring. Fritz developed other methods to elicit expressions of emotion such as role playing significant people in our lives, including ourselves in all kinds of situations. He understood that releasing deep feelings that have been repressed, opens us to more of our potential aliveness.

BELIEFS

We know that as children most of us take on the beliefs of those around us. This process is referred to in Gestalt as introjection. We "swallow whole" beliefs without chewing them first to find out if they taste ok, whether parts of them are ok, but other parts make us sick, etc. Usually this process occurs without our awareness. We may go along with our family's prejudices about other groups of people, for example, or go along with their spiritual and religious beliefs. Children often don't question these until something shakes these introjected beliefs to the core: falling in love with someone who is a member of a group our parents disapprove of, for example. But often we miss a lot of these introjections. They manifest as "shoulds" and "should nots". So growing up we hopefully become more aware of which beliefs fit us and which don't. There have been a number of occasions when clients have felt nauseated on discovering beliefs that they didn't *taste* first. And they have often vomited these up both literally and figuratively once they become aware of them.

Apart from revising our beliefs to fit us more accurately as we become more aware, there is also the issue of our beliefs being rigid, and there being no room for change. This black and white thinking can limit who we are. It is like a suit of armor we wear on top of our constantly-in-motion physical, mental and emotional self. Some of these expectations become cultural mandates. For example I've heard that in Japan achieving success is so important that children are severely pressured to get top grades and their parents are pressured to push them. Many of these children become tense, sick and emotionally troubled. The aliveness in these children is shut down. To handle this serious dilemma, a number of Japanese parents decided to send their children to school in California where the academic and social pressure is less and where they can be more themselves, more alive, vibrant and creative.

EXPECTATIONS IN RELATIONSHIPS

Expectations and beliefs often mean the same thing. It is helpful to look at our expectations for ourselves and for those we spend time with, like our partners and children. Often expectations are out of our awareness, and when others don't follow through as we expect they *should,* we get angry, upset, and often go into blaming the other or ourselves.

I've heard in earlier generations expectations in families were more clearly defined as the roles of family members were clearer. Now every time two people join, they bring with them different expectations from their families of origin as well as from whatever work they've done on themselves to change these. Wherever they are, there is usually a lot to discover to come to some workable understanding of how to live together.

RIGID BELIEFS AND EXPECTATIONS

As is true of expectations, beliefs are often out of awareness, too, whether these are thoughts, feelings, ideas, sensations or creative experiences. We often don't become aware of them until we meet up with those who have different beliefs.

Rigid beliefs are those which feel necessary for our survival or our identity. To give them up would threaten our sense of self. So we hang on to them tenaciously. For example, some people have the rigid belief that something is wrong with them if they feel attracted to someone other than their partner. They would be willing to squelch their aliveness. If they were less rigid about this, they might accept these feelings as normal and natural, but choose not to act on them. In this way they are honoring their nature and allowing it to be without acting on it. And of course a third way is to revise their belief to accept acting on these feelings and to accept the consequences.

So there are many dimensions to this theme. As we know, nothing is easy or simple. Our beliefs are constantly being challenged, rigid or not, so being aware of them and willing to explore them is an important step in our growth and awareness.

EXPERIMENTS
1. *Make a list of some of your major beliefs about your values, relationships, work, spirituality, and health.*
2. *Note if there are some you feel flexible about and some you could never change.*
3. *Do any of these limit your aliveness? Which ones?*
4. *Are you willing to explore, modify or change any of these?*

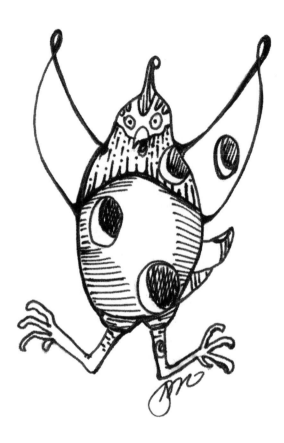

There are holes in our personality.

7. THE HOLES IN OUR PERSONALITY

"We are like a piece of Swiss cheese." – Fritz Perls

Founder Fritz Perls saw the human being as having many aspects and qualities, some of which are foreground one moment and background the next. We are constantly moving and changing and yet usually always recognizable. During our lifetimes many of us hide and disown parts of ourselves. Sometimes we lose parts, give them away or they are taken from us.

Enjoying being graphic, Fritz likened us to a piece of Swiss cheese, with many holes. Through awareness we hopefully will re-own and integrate our missing parts with the rest of our personality. When the holes in our piece of cheese get filled in, we become whole again.

These aspects could be qualities we don't like about ourselves, such as our timidity, jealousy, anger or hurt. But also they could be qualities we respect and care about. For example many feel they have given their love to someone else, and didn't get it back once the relationship ended. Sometimes people experience gaping holes in themselves following the loss of a loved one. I have often heard from a client "I'm afraid to look inside; part of me is gone, and I don't know who I am anymore."

In a Gestalt workshop I attended in the 60s at Esalen Institute in Big Sur, California, Fritz decided he wanted to do some personal work on himself. He asked his co-leader, Jim Simkin, to work with him. (This is not uncommon for Gestalt therapists to work on themselves in front of their training groups to model being open when appropriate.) Fritz had been in psychoanalytic training in Berlin during Freud's time and had written a paper for one of the conferences, which Freud had not accepted. Some 50 years later Fritz finally decided to work on this piece of unfinished business with Freud. During the session, Jim asked him to put Freud on the empty chair and talk to him. Fritz' hurt and pain poured out, and he cried deeply for some time. This part of Fritz, hidden away inside of himself, finally emerged, and this hole in his personality was filled up again. He felt very relieved after the session.

Shamans, indigenous healers, often retrieve lost parts of their subjects. The Gestalt approach, which to me is similar, invites us to seek our own missing selves and to re-integrate them. This can be done by engaging them in dialogue through role playing or writing a script and getting to know them.

EXPERIMENTS

1. *List aspects of yourself that you have hidden, lost, disowned or were taken from you. (See above for suggestions)*

2. *Are you able to embrace & accept these aspects of yourself? Even if you have judgments about them you will begin the process of integrating them back into you. For example, one person owned her anger at her children. Another owned her habit of lying.*

3. *Ask yourself how you feel right after doing this as well as a few days or weeks later. You may wish to do this more than once.*

This process of re-owning is related to telling ourselves the truth (Chapter: Telling Ourselves Our Truth?), which is an important part of being whole. We don't have to like parts of ourselves, but we do have to accept them.

8. RESPONSIBILITY

"Re-spond-ability is the ability to respond." – Fritz Perls

WE ARE RESPONSIBLE FOR OURSELVES

In essence we are responsible for our feelings, thoughts and actions. Others may influence us, but they are not responsible... Thus our parents aren't to blame for how we turned out, nor are they to accept credit for how we turned out. They did influence us and we took on what we wished from them and rejected what we didn't want, even though it was often out of our awareness at the time.

Now one of the greatest tasks in life is developing our awareness. Then being responsible for ourselves becomes a more conscious process.

Fritz believed that many people do not want to grow up and take responsibility for their lives. He felt we would rather continue blaming and manipulating others, as we did as children. So a lot of the awareness is about seeing the games that we play. Many of us are afraid of taking care of ourselves, taking responsibility for our lives. To put it another way, we are afraid of moving from environmental support to self support, which we all do when we mature.

Years ago a client I was working with got in touch with the coy little girl she played to get what she wanted in life. Giving this successful role up wasn't easy. It meant taking responsibility for asking for what she wanted, rather than manipulating. And it meant being open to being told 'no', which was the most difficult part. During a workshop she said goodbye to this part of herself and the sobs were deep, long and releasing. Now, many years later, she is a successful organizer and leader in her community. Her changes are profound.

WE ARE NOT RESPONSIBLE FOR OTHERS

The opposite is now important to consider, and that is we are not responsible for those in our lives. How many of you think it is your *fault* that your partner left, that your children are having difficulties, or that your parents are failing. As for you therapists and counselors, how responsible do you feel for your clients?

The role of the rescuer, the people helper, the placator are often based on feeling better off than others, often like a topdog. This attitude can demean and discount them. There is an arrogance in this stance. When others don't appreciate all that is being done for them, it is worth taking a look at the attitude of the rescuers, who may see themselves as better than those they are presuming to help. Also in this role, we don't have to reveal ourselves as *you* are the problem, not us. And to make matters even worse, the rescuer needs to find some victims to help, to make themselves feel important! You see this dynamic not only in marriages, families, therapy relationships, but in organizations and nations as well. It is hierarchical and authoritarian and it does not honor egalitarian relationships. It provokes the underdog to come out swinging at the topdog.

Steve Karpman, MD, a Transactional Analyst, whom I worked together with in the 60s at the US Naval Hospital in Oakland, California, devised a process he called The Drama Triangle, which identifies the perpetrator, the victim and the rescuer in many situations. The rescuer is as dysfunctional as all the other roles, so counselors, beware. When I was in training with Jim Simkin in the 60s he made sure to confront me about my tendencies to rescue others, and luckily I found out how to be there for others without rescuing or *trying* to rescue them. Fritz Perls taught me how to believe that each person had within themselves their own truth, and no therapist could interpret or provide that for another. Honoring everyone's inner knowing, for which they can take proud responsibility, is the most important outcome of letting go of the rescuer role.

EXPERIMENTS

1. *Get in touch with some of your favorite childhood ways (other than by being clear and direct) of getting others to take care of you, such as getting them to buy you toys or take you to the zoo. As grown ups get in touch with some of your favorite ways to convince others to pay your way, take you out, clean your house, give you a job, etc. For example maybe you were demanding, played the victim, whined, threatened, withheld what the other wanted, used charm, etc.*

2. *How have these helped you over the years. Or have they?*

3. *Experiment not using these manipulations. How is it?*

Lose your mind and come to your senses.

Section C

GET OUT OF YOUR HEAD*

1. **Lose your Mind and Come to your Senses**

2. **We are the Image Makers**

3. **The Fitting Game**

4. **Thinking in Concepts, Generalities and Theories**

5. **Problems of Labeling**

*If you feel challenged doing the experiments in this section of the book, please read the chapter in **Section F: How All of These Practices Relate to Gestalt Therapy.**

1. LOSE YOUR MIND AND COME TO YOUR SENSES*

"We can spend our whole lives escaping from the monsters of our minds."
– Pema Chodron, Buddhist author and teacher

As infants we experienced our world through our bodies and senses. We hadn't learned a language yet, and we hadn't honed our thinking skills yet! Do you remember what it was like back then? Maybe this experiment will help you remember. Please do this before reading further.

EXPERIMENT

1. *Close your eyes. Imagine you are an infant in a garden on a nice day. You have not learned any words yet. Experience the garden through your senses. Do this for a few minutes.*

2. *Now imagine an adult such as one of your parents comes to sit beside you in the garden and begins teaching you words for what you are seeing, hearing, smelling, tasting and touching: this is a BUTTERFLY; that is a FLOWER; the SUN is what shines on us; that is the WIND blowing on us, etc.*

3. *Keep your eyes closed and experience both situations for a moment longer. Now slowly open your eyes. What are you aware of? Were these two states different for you? How?*

I have invited a number of people in my classes to do this experiment over the years. Many could not experience the garden without words. They thought of words as they were experiencing their senses. Those that could do the first part of the experiment without words, had some powerful experiences as they enjoyed the sounds, quiet, colors, wind, sun, shapes, smells, textures, tastes and the movement of things. Others were happy to learn words to put on their experiences, but they did detract somewhat from the

* Fritz Perls quote

experience. Others lost track of experiencing the garden and focused more on reacting to the parent who was teaching them the words.

Being able to sense without language and thoughts can be a very important experience. Artists probably know how to do this more than the rest of us, except of course, infants.

THE GOD OF RATIONALITY

In school we are taught to use our mind and think things through. We learn to set goals and work towards these to get what we want in life. These activities require us to think, plan, and act. Then we'll be successful, we're told. Much of our adult life requires these abilities. We learn to conceptualize, evaluate, summarize, categorize and theorize at great length. The impression many of us got growing up is that these were the only things that were important in life. Doing these things well was rewarded with good grades. Many received labels of being 'smart' or 'intellectual' and many developed careers relying solely on these skills.

OUR LOST SOULS

What happened to our intuitive side? Our playful side? Our feelings and emotional side? Our souls? Our creativity? These aspects were treated like second class citizens in school, and in many schools they didn't even exist. Our society and culture didn't get it.

When Fritz moved from New York City to the West Coast of the US in the mid 1960s, he spent a lot of his time demonstrating to those of us in his workshops how much we were "in our heads" and out of touch with the rest of ourselves and the world around us. He noticed what we were doing to ourselves. To him it was *obvious* that we weren't whole integrated human beings; we were too much in our heads, and we were out of touch with our feelings and our bodies.

He noticed how hard it was for many of us to allow whatever wanted to emerge to come forth—without controlling the process. He saw how rigid we were. He saw our lack of valuing our emotional life. "I want to turn paper people into real people" Fritz said when he first came to the West Coast from New York City. At that time sociological books about these notions were in vogue. *The Man in the Grey Flannel Suit* by Sloan Wilson, and *The Lonely Crowd* by David Riesman, were among the list.

In addition to the many things going on during the 60s, marijuana and psychedelics came to the fore. Having been in the San Francisco area at this time as a young social worker, I can attest that many of my colleagues and I were hungry for more intuitive, spiritual, right brained knowing, which these substances provided. Some of us experimented with these under controlled circumstances with professional guidance. Our left brained thinking would disappear for a number of hours as we opened up to our own unresolved psychological issues as well as the mysteries of the universe, which then opened the doors to the many spiritual disciplines and humanistic therapies that emerged at that time. It was a profound time and luckily we were able to explore the depths of these experiences in Gestalt therapy.

SPEAKING SPECIFICALLY, IN DETAIL, IN THE PRESENT TENSE, WITH FEELING

In his workshops, Fritz kept directing our attention to the details of our experiences and to our feelings about them, rather than to our general stories about ourselves, including our interpretations and theories about why we behaved the way we did.

He caught us speaking in the third person saying *"one* feels…", or "after awhile *you* begin to feel…", rather than *"I* feel". The Human Potential Movement, of which he was a main contributor, changed all that by encouraging people to speak in the present tense and to include their feelings. After much trial and error, we eventually got it. This seemingly small and specific example began to change the face of personal communication among many people, from schools to the human potential culture in general. Since many came to California from Asia, South America and Europe to train with Fritz and other Gestalt trainers, these practices were taught in many countries and translated into many languages as well.

I recall a Chinese social worker in San Francisco, who was working on her anger at her parents in a Gestalt training group I was leading. When I asked her if she would be more comfortable speaking in Chinese to please do so, she said "Oh, no, I could never get angry at them in Chinese, but in English it is ok!"

So gradually people around the new therapies began speaking from their feelings and using *I* rather than *you* or *one*. People were coming into their senses more and more. It was at this time that Fritz coined the phrase "Lose your mind and come to your senses", which became a mantra for the new learnings.

Unfortunately other addictions such as alcohol and the hard drugs like heroin became popular with some who couldn't tolerate their lives. They used these to cover up the pain of their critical minds which were constantly judging them for legitimate and not so legitimate behaviors.

EXPERIMENT
Close your eyes. Feel your feet on the floor. Sense what your feet want to do. Stay with them. Allow them to move you rather than you moving them. Try the same thing with one hand. Where does it take you. Try it with your eyes. Where do they want to go.

Now allow whatever wants to emerge. As I do this now, my feet moved me to the window, where I see the snow covering more and more of my garden and I notice the thermometer says 28 degrees outside. Now my feet move to the door. I go outside and experience that special quietness when it is snowing. To me this quiet is magical. Then my feet take me to my car. My rational mind has swung into gear, and I put my car in the garage away from the falling snow. Then I go back out into the quiet again.

Take a break from your usual logical thinking; take a deep breath and notice the surprises that emerge when you don't control your silence. Savor these experiences.

2. WE ARE THE IMAGE MAKERS

"Living up to an image that you have of yourself or that other people have of you is inauthentic living." – Eckhart Tolle, The New Earth

THE STORIES WE TELL OURSELVES

Some people live in their minds more than their bodies, and the stories they tell themselves often don't match how others experience them.

A man has an image of his wife as strong and out to hurt him by her behavior. This is the story he tells himself about her. If he would take the time to observe her very closely he would see her fear and vulnerability. He is used to making up stories and images in his mind to explain his experience of her, rather than literally looking at her. He does the same to himself—makes up a story to explain himself to himself. He is out of touch with his senses regarding his wife as well as himself. And he is isolated and lonely.

In 1966 my husband at the time and I attended a workshop with Fritz Perls, at Esalen Institute in Big Sur California. During our work with him, Fritz asked us to sit opposite one another, close our eyes and create an image of the other in our minds. Then he asked us to open our eyes, look very closely at each other and describe what we experienced in detail. In both cases, what we experienced was a far cry from the one dimensional image we each had of the other in our minds. Our "perfect" image of one another didn't allow for our complexities, or for the fact that we were rarely the same from moment to moment. That was almost 50 years ago, and I'm still deeply affected by that experience.

EXPERIMENT
Describe an image you have of someone important to you. Now put aside this image and begin to look at this person's multi-dimensionality. Allow yourself to see aspects you haven't seen before even if you judge them.

NOT WANTING TO SEE AND HEAR

Many of us don't want to see and hear clearly, as we may see something we don't want to see. And doing so might bring up a lot of unpleasant feelings and attitudes we'd rather not experience.

Seeing a person clearly and then accepting him for all of who he is, is difficult for many of us. So we think finding reasons for someone's behavior will take care of that: "Oh he had a very troubled childhood which is why he is isn't always nice". If we told the truth we would describe his behavior, and leave out his justifications. We might just say, "He often yells at me and hits me, especially when he is drinking."

WANTING TO CHANGE OUR PARTNER

If we acknowledge this person's "negative aspects", we might also try to change him. Many of us like to be helpful, so we may make it our job to help the other person change. However, this topdog role can make the other feel put down and resentful. We often try to change the other to make ourselves feel better or to have our partner measure up to our *image* of him, rather than to genuinely help him. "You don't eat enough healthy food." (I want my partner to be able to care for me in old age.) "You should be more spiritual." (I want someone to attend spiritual events with.) "You shouldn't be angry."(I want everyone to see my partner as kind and loving.) And on and on!

CREATING IMAGES OF OTHERS

Often when we first fall in love, we put all "negative" qualities we see and hear in the background, and focus on the "positive" qualities we love. Then we create an image of how this person is going to meet our needs. Have you ever done this and found out later how many observations of your partner you pushed under the rug? We mistake our image for the real person, who is much more complex and intricate than our ideal image has allowed.

For example, "He is shy," they said of my father. The truth was that when I looked at him closely he clenched his jaw, and on occasion would let it slip that he didn't like a lot of people, that he was quite judgmental, which he didn't want others to know. So he hid behind his shy image, which we liked as we didn't want the truth out about him either!

Gestalt practices emphasize learning to see and hear with precision and specificity, and to become aware of the stories and justifications we create in our minds to explain what we don't want to see and hear.

Our stories are challenged by life. For example, a man told his wife he didn't want to be married anymore. She was in shock, as her image of him was that he was a loving and devoted husband who would occasionally feel down. She did not listen to him or see him clearly when he told her of his unhappiness. Instead she told herself that "he will be all right in a day or two," which fit into her image of him. When he left she went into shock. She didn't take him seriously.

In the 70s at a workshop I facilitated, there was a man who rarely looked directly at others. He put his head back slightly and looked down a little. As a minister he was used to looking down at his congregation. During an experiment participants sat across from their spouses. I noticed the minister looking down at his wife of 25 years, so I took a piece of scotch tape and attached it to his chin and chest so that he was looking directly at her. The tape pulled each time he attempted to tilt his head back to his more comfortable position. He became aware of his posture and eventually looked directly at her, and then suddenly he exclaimed that he didn't recognize her. He was visibly shaken. He had never taken the time to see her fully. As a result of this seemingly simple experiment, he went into a state of shock. Later he saw a therapist in his community to help him with this frightening experience.

As a therapist I often hear from clients "My partner doesn't know who I really am", or "She doesn't see me clearly." We often hear women say "He sees me as just a sex object" or "a mother who takes care of him". One time the ex-husband of a client who came to one of her sessions with me, screamed at her "All you ever saw me as was a stud to give you children, when you knew I didn't want any!" She had never taken him seriously, never really listened to him, as it didn't fit her *image* of the husband she wanted for herself. She plugged him into her "husband box" and ignored her experience of him.

All of these mind games we play overshadow our seeing, hearing and experiencing the truth about ourselves and others.

BEING PRESENT

Being out of touch with our senses and only in touch with our mind and its false images can lead to incredible loneliness and dissociation. Being authentic and relating to a real person changes all of that loneliness into contact and aliveness.

Seeing and hearing clearly and accurately over months and years, as well as observing details, can take a lot of time, but if we want to be connected with others, and have a meaningful life, we must learn to observe, watch, and notice the minutia as well as the big picture. We need to learn to be fully present, without judgment at these times.

EXPERIMENTS

1. *In a group or while people-watching sometime, look around and purposely create an image of each one. For example," the lady in the worn out dress is homeless and probably crazy" or "that handsome man is probably unable to settle down with one woman." Make up lots of stories on purpose; exaggerate them. This will help you become more aware of story telling and image making in the future.*

2. *Take 5 minutes without talking to look and listen to someone you are close to. Be aware of your mind getting in the way by making images of the person. Just look and listen. Be present with all of you.*

3. *Then ask this friend if he feels you see him clearly. Ask him how you don't see him fully. Have you misunderstood him? Have you put labels on him that don't fit? Ask him to help you see him more clearly.*

Of course we also create limiting images of ourselves, and at some point in life we get challenged. Then we can't get away with our own self image. This can lead to panic for some, who have no inner sense of who they are—they have no inner self support. Others have less difficulty being challenged.

Years ago a young, attractive mother came to see me. She had always been seen as a competent and loving person, which she happily adopted as her self image. Her presenting problem was that she had 2 children under 3 who constantly pushed her buttons, messing up her carefully kept home and provoking her anger. Her self image didn't have room for anger or messiness! She was anxious and frantic. And of course she wanted me to help her keep her *nice person image* by giving her some strategies to change her children. I suggested instead that it might be useful for her to work on herself to become more accepting of them, which in the long run, would calm her children down.

So creating limiting images which don't begin to encompass all of who we are prevents us from seeing and hearing accurately, causing us to be isolated, superficial, and out of contact with ourselves and others. The speediness with which we create these images, is like the quick media sound bites we have of one another. Nothing but superficial contact can happen with this approach to ourselves and to others. Having deep emotions can be avoided as well. We don't have to feel all of our feelings, or those of others, and we don't have to bother to work through a lot of our issues which all these feelings might provoke. Avoiding this pain means we cannot experience the joys of deep connecting.

3. THE FITTING GAME

"The incessant mental noise of thinking prevents you from finding
that realm of inner stillness that is inseparable from Being."
– Eckhart Tolle, The Power of Now

Fritz loved games. Apart from his favorite, chess, he loved to create Gestalt games such as the Fitting Game.

Since we are in our minds so much; and since our educational system has encouraged us to develop our minds often at the exclusion of everything else, we have become masters and mistresses of theory making about who we are, what we are like inside and outside, why we behave the way we do, and so on.

In the field of therapy and counseling, professionals spend years developing theories to explain behavior, feeling and thinking states. The book, the DSM IV is the psychiatric bible of diagnoses. We just have to review the book to see which label we "fit into" and which label those we know "fit into". This is the game—figuring out who fits where.

Fritz used to tease us if we played this game in his workshops. We were definitely in our heads, figuring things out, rather than in the present experiencing ourselves and the others in the here and now.

And clients love to play this game as well. "The reason I behave this way is because I am narcissistic." "You are depressed." "This diagnosis fits me perfectly."

I can picture a therapist looking at the DSM IV, scratching his head and looking at the ceiling while a client sits waiting for her to look at him and say something, or make some kind of human contact. Psychiatrists and therapists often do this when they diagnose a client. Do you fit in the "depressed" box? Do you fit into the "normal" box, whatever that is.

And there are numerous other schemata that people love to play with. Many psychological books that come out are filled with new categories to put people into. Much time is spent seeing which label fits us. Then there are the Astrological signs, political party affiliations, religious and spiritual orientations, and the Enneagram categories. I think you get the picture. These are interesting parlor games, and sometimes useful. However, be aware of how much these tasks invite you to be in your head!

And of course, like I mentioned earlier, a label is a sound bite, which only describes a small part of who we are. It can promote superficial understanding and obscure how complex and intricate we all are. (See Chapter C5: *The Problems of Labeling.*)

EXPERIMENTS

1. *Think of a time when you and friends "tried to figure someone out". What labels did you come up with for this person, or what theories did you uncover to explain this person. Did it help your relationship with this person? How?*

2. *Ask yourself if you identify with a community group: the soccer club, the spiritual group, the political group, the book club, etc. Notice your process as you "figure out" which group you choose. Ask yourself which aspects of yourself you will have to subdue or hide to be involved with each of the groups you are considering.*

3. *To become more aware of playing this game, do it on purpose, exaggerate it so you can see it more clearly. Make it silly and fun.*

Since we are all very complex with many aspects and qualities, it is almost impossible to fit ourselves into a box or category without having to *limit* ourselves. This process is *very harmful* to seeing and hearing each other clearly. We can't "be present" with one another if we are playing the fitting game, as we will be in our heads trying to fit each person into a box in our minds, and we will miss the subtle nuances of the person in front of us. We won't be present and therefore we won't be able to experience the other fully.

4. THINKING IN CONCEPTS, GENERALITIES AND THEORIES

*"Can you look without the voice in your head commenting,
drawing conclusions, comparing or trying to figure something out?"*
– Eckhart Tolle, The New Earth

Have you ever met anyone who has difficulty being specific? Someone who, when you ask them how they are, goes into a general theory? "I'm in an impasse now, between the old me and the new me," or "I'm getting a handle on my histrionic self."

These folks learned how to generalize and theorize in school. Of course we all got good grades for learning how to do that well. I was taught that these qualities were signs that our culture was intellectual, sophisticated and civilized! And that uncivilized societies, such as indigenous cultures, must be the opposite. They were too concrete (read 'specific').

After many years of living with the Gestalt command, "Describe your experience in minute detail," I learned to pay attention to the specifics of my experience. If I looked at you and said " You look sad," Fritz would say, "What did you see that led to you to conclude that this person is sad?" "Well, his mouth is turned down, his eyes are looking down, and as I look closer I see tears." "Now you are seeing," Fritz would say, "and not just imagining."

So, much of Gestalt practice is about slowing down and seeing and hearing what we experience in the here and now. And then noticing the theories or imaginings or interpretations we developed to explain them.

A pet peeve of mine is the frequent greeting, "How is your day going so far?", which immediately invites the person to go into his head and generalize about how he is: I'm good, I'm distracted. I'm having a bad day, etc. Rarely do we go into specifics with these questions, since they are often just a greeting. However, these constant questions train us to constantly go into our head, evaluate and generalize about ourselves. And then we carry this habit forward to do the same with others.

For me it is disconcerting when I am in the moment with this person, and then they ask me how my day is going. I leave the moment, go into my head to summarize how my day is going so far and I usually feel like I don't want to answer the question, unless it is someone I know. The point is I leave the here and now. And since it is just a greeting, there may not be time to go into specifics if I so wished. Although I personally don't like this question from strangers, many people like this greeting. I'm bringing this up to invite you to be more aware.

On another note we often misinterpret what we experience. Let's say you see a woman whose mouth turns up as she looks at you. "Ah, she is smiling at me" you say to yourself. Nice try. But if you look closer at her mouth, you might see her clenched jaw. You can't know what interpretation to put on that without asking her. Is she upset with you? Is she having a bad day and covering it up with a phony smile? Again, we have a tendency to assume meaning to specifics of what we see.

The bottom line is we go from experiencing to interpreting *so quickly* that we aren't aware of what we are doing. Because we move so fast we end up experiencing the interpretations our minds create rather than what we experience with our senses, which precede our interpretations. Again, the message here is to become more aware. (See the chapter called *Slow Down; You Move Too Fast.*)

Why bother, you ask? One of the most common mistakes we human folks make, unlike the 4-leggeds, is that we often misinterpret what we experience. If we are out of alignment, riddled with unfinished business, rushing, distracted we most likely will misinterpret our specific phenomenological experiences. How often have the speedy smart alecks in your life incorrectly finished your sentences for you? Or how often have you been the smart aleck and done this to others? Being in our heads creating concepts, interpretations, and theories prevents us from being in the here and now with each other. A common experience I appreciated about the Navajos was that they didn't greet one another with a question as they felt it was intrusive. Instead they shook one another's hand and said: Good Morning, Good Afternoon, or Good Evening. This did not invite us to evaluate ourselves or answer a question we might not wish to answer!

EXPERIMENTS

1. *Look at someone. Quickly generalize about what you see. Do this again with another, and then another. Exaggerate this process. For example, "He is a right wing conservative snob"; "She is a whiny liberal who feels like a victim all the time," etc.*

2. *Do the experiment again, at a slower pace. Now notice what specific observations (that you saw or heard) led to your generalization.*

5. THE PROBLEMS OF LABELING

"Observe how the mind labels an unpleasant moment and how this labeling process, this continuous sitting in judgment, creates pain and unhappiness." – Eckhart Tolle, The Power of Now

Labels and words are short cuts to understanding. We have been praised for our ability to think quickly and make generalizations from what we think are facts.

LABELS CREATE A CULTURE OF SUPERFICIALITY

Often these generalizations (labels, judgments) are superficial and don't begin to address the complexities of each person. And these labels are "fixed" nouns, ignoring the fact that we are constantly in motion, moving and changing moment to moment, as is our world. Some indigenous languages, such as Navajo, have fewer nouns and more verbs to honor this dynamic. Their language is more congruent with life than other languages.

In our families we might be labeled the troublemaker, the withdrawn one, the cute one, the smart one. Our society might call us the young one, the old one. Racial and ethnic labels abound everywhere. The psychiatric bible, the DSM-IV, is full of diagnostic labels. Alcoholics Anonymous invites its members to label themselves. Horoscopes label. "I'm schizophrenic"; "I'm an alcoholic", "I'm a Pisces".

It is presumed that we know what these labels mean, and can have a good sense of a person by just knowing the labels. To some extent this can be true. However, we sometimes believe these labels are "all of us".

I've seen a number of clients who were afraid to look into their inner self, below their labels, exclaiming that "I'm afraid there is nothing there". These labels can be devastating, particularly for young people, who rely on peer appreciation for their identity. These people haven't formed a sense of self which is solid, flexible and fluid.

LABELING THE LABELS POSITIVE OR NEGATIVE

Then we often get into labeling the labels! Are they negative or positive labels, whatever those mean? Of course this is in the eyes of the beholder: what you experience as negative others may not. For example, if someone is able to express grief fully, some people may see this as a negative. Others might call this positive, as this person has the ability to feel deeply and to release their pain.

Have you noticed how quickly people add a positive or negative to whatever is being discussed. For example, "You're being negative" if someone says they are concerned about climate change. The implication here is that the person is being negative, and shouldn't be. To another person, they might praise the person for paying attention to the climate and pursuing ways to deal with it or move to a new location. This relates to an early story about Fritz and Lore Perls. They were aware of the Nazis coming after them, and said so. Colleagues suggested they were being negative. The Perls escaped. Some of their Jewish colleagues didn't. So who is positive and who is negative? To me this is more about awareness and unawareness.

Positive labels can be just as problematic as negative ones. Some may feel the positive labels aren't true and are manipulations by the parents or society to "build up self esteem"; others may feel scared that they can't live up to them. I've worked with a number of clients over the years that were raised to feel they were *special*. This label became very troubling for them as they felt they had to live up to some *ideal image* for their families. They experienced a lot of pressure and stress from themselves, of course, but from others as well. Realizing the label did not cover all of who they were was helpful in accepting themselves.

An example I see frequently is the person who "tries hard" to be positive all the time. For starters this person is often seen by others as superficial and unreal. But more importantly this feeling that they *should* be positive all the time means they have to sublimate important aspects of themselves including their fears, upsets, sadness and anger. Barbara Ehrenreich's book *Bright-sided: How the Relentless Promotion of Positive Thinking has Undermined America,* describes the dangers of not seeing ourselves clearly and truthfully.

THE LABELS OF HOPELESS AND HOPEFUL

This is also true of judging things as either *hopeful or hopeless*. Both of these are labels about our experience, and can distract us from the truth of what we are experiencing. If I have to convince myself that things are hopeful, I may not see the danger signs, may not pay attention to my inner experience which tells me to do something different. Labeling something as hopeless is also restricting my experience, as it is a generalization that can cause me to be depressed. Taking these labels out of my vocabulary allows me to experience *what is* without my mind adding another generalized dimension.

We are full human beings who have the ability to feel, and learn from all of our experiences. Hiding aspects of ourselves is depriving ourselves of knowing our truth. And usually doing this doesn't solve the problem, as those aspects, such as our anger and fear, will emerge somewhere else in our bodies or psyches, often as tensions and illnesses. Pema Chodron, Buddhist author and teacher, has said "Hope robs us of the present moment."

EXPERIMENTS

1. *Exaggerate labeling yourself. Write them down.*

2. *Do the same about a friend or spouse. Again, write them down.*

3. *Ask yourself of what value labeling is to you.*

When I ask myself this question I see that judging and labeling someone (to myself) keeps me at a distance from them, something I sometimes want. This was a revelation to me, and now I can take the distance I need without labeling others as much.

I often hear people quickly label something as "negative". The same is true of the label "fear". And then they dismiss these experiences by saying something like "don't go there," and move on in the blink of an eye. They *disown* these experiences rather than exploring them.

The result of all this labeling is that we learn to see ourselves and others as labels and not as full human beings. Labeling is a mental activity, keeping us out of touch with our sensations, feelings and inner awareness. And it leads to a superficial sense of who we are, as well as to dysfunctional behaviors and a life of dissatisfaction.

People are hungry for a deeper connection with one another. Loneliness and depression are two constants in surveys we take. We ask people at gatherings about consciousness and personal growth, what they want most in their lives. Their responses are 1) to be seen and heard as unique beings, and 2) to experience the love and caring that comes from deep knowing and understanding.

Certainly the world might be better off if we never labeled, but that is unlikely to happen. Rather, see this tendency as something to become more aware of, something to do less often, and more importantly as a reason to describe in detail without judgment more often! Remember positive labeling is labeling too, and can diminish the person by not seeing them fully.

Deep Feelings.

Section D

AUTHENTICITY*

1. **The Here and Now**

2. **Deep Feelings**

3. **Vulnerability**

4. **Being Direct**

5. **Contact and Withdrawal**

6. **Congruence**

*If you feel challenged doing the experiments in this section of the book, please read the chapter in **Section F: How All of these Practices relate to Gestalt Therapy.**

1. BEING IN THE HERE AND NOW

"Be Here Now," – *Ram Das*

"The birth of a man is the birth of his sorrow... He lives for what is always out of reach. His thirst to survival in the future makes him incapable of living in the present." – *Chuang Tzu, Chinese philosopher*

I watched an ad on TV about a family on an outing in the country. The dad was watching the road, but also the TV on the dashboard. His wife was reading a book. One kid was texting a friend. Another had earphones on watching an iPod cartoon. Then I recalled a trip to Europe I helped facilitate for teenagers in 1960. While driving a VW bus through the Alps a few of the kids in the back seat were reading comic books. Then I remembered a client addicted to video games who was afraid to meet real people. And I talked with a counselor at a university counseling clinic, who described many of her clients as isolated and lonely, and who didn't know how to relate to others, only those from their past via emails, skyping and texting.

We are all hopeless, I thought. So many of us don't see and hear what is right in front of us. I thought things had gotten better since the 60s, but I think they have gotten worse, as there are more than books to distract us now. Since I was doing a lot of thinking, I then asked myself how I was feeling about it all. And I got in touch with how very sad I had become, thinking of so many lost souls who haven't yet found the joys and sorrows of living more in the present.

Then, still sad, I look out of my window. I notice the large grape leaves, and the many different shades of green in the trees, ground cover and bushes. The new persimmon tree is bending with the wind. The hops vine is stretching to expand across the trellis. The sky is many shades of grey and white, and I see a large patch of blue. The water hose is snaking its way across the lawn, and all the plants look plump and healthy. As I take in all of this, as I drink it in and savor it, I feel grateful and renewed in this moment. Then

I smell gasoline as I hear a truck braking on the highway hill not far away. I grimace and hold my nose. The sound of the truck dissipates as it moves on, and so does the smell. I turn back to my computer, here now, typing this sentence. I *shuttle* back and forth from the thoughts of how difficult it is to be in the here and now, and how sad it is for so many and the beauty and ugliness around me, off and on, as life goes on.

WHAT DISTRACTS US FROM BEING IN THE HERE AND NOW

There are a myriad of ways we distract ourselves. You'll probably recognize many of these.

- Being busy
- Going fast
- Tensing ourselves and distorting our postures so we don't feel too much
- Our unresolved issues from the past
- Conceptualizing, evaluating, judging, generalizing, theorizing: being stuck in our minds
- Focusing on power, fortune & fame
- Belief that there is nothing inside of us and we're not *ok*
- Belief that a counselor or spiritual teacher knows best, and that I don't
- Overly working & overly playing
- Indulging our addictions
- Looking for a quick fix to everything that bothers us about our health, work, relationships, spirituality including medication
- Our disturbing emotions such as self consciousness, jealousy, envy, embarrassment, shame and guilt
- Fear of the unknown, of losing what we have, of not getting what we want
- Experiencing unfamiliar sensations

As you can see, we can spend our whole lives being distracted. So what is the problem if we distract ourselves? To do this all the time or even part of the time, we'd have to ignore our inner being and our inner knowing. And who wants to be stuck in any of the above dynamics? We'd be a mess after awhile. So why do we avoid the present so much? What are we afraid of?

FEAR OF BEING IN THE HERE AND NOW

Yes, many are afraid of being in the present. We might lose control and feel feelings we don't want to feel. Or some unresolved issues might pop into our awareness, which we want to avoid. Or we might get upset seeing the seamy side of life and get depressed. As we all know, there is a huge number of people now who are taking anti-depressants, including children.

Years ago a 35 year old Navajo woman, whom I worked with at the Indian Health Service, became afraid during an exercise where I asked the class to go inside themselves. She said she had never done that. Ever since she was a child she was taught that the minute the sun came up to jump out of bed, put on her shoes, run outside to greet the sun, and not to take her shoes off until she went to bed that night. All day she was busy tending the sheep, going to school, helping her mother cook and clean. There were no skeletons in her closet that I could find, as I knew her well; going inside was something she had never done before and she experienced strange sensations when she did so.

Many people don't know how to deal with their experiences of being in the here and now, other than through avoidance, distraction and denial. The popularity of meditation practices over the last 40 years has helped a lot of people. A good therapist with an existential or transpersonal orientation such as a Gestalt person, can guide people into finding ways to go inside where they will probably face the truth of the world and their own lives in a way that enriches them rather than restricting their genuine aliveness.

EXPERIMENTS

1. *Exaggerate for a minute or two NOT paying attention to the here and now. Stay in your mind: thinking, watching TV, reading, texting, etc. Notice your breathing.*

2. *Now do the reverse: put your mind distractions in an imaginary box next to you and now pay attention to what you see, hear, sense, smell, taste and touch. Notice your breathing. Allow for the good, the bad and everything in between.*

3. *Describe your experience doing both. Practice this often.*

2. DEEP FEELINGS

"Feelings will get you closer to the truth of who you are than thinking."
– Eckhart Tolle, The Power of Now

None of us may wish to feel the deep wrenching feelings that arise occasionally during our lifetimes. We don't want to experience them as we imagine it will be painful, or we think we *shouldn't* feel them. Many say that fighting our feelings is more painful than feeling them.

There is a difference between experiencing a feeling and expressing it. I can know that deep inside I'm feeling angry, which is different than my telling someone *about* it, or *expressing* it.

Fritz used to talk about grief, rage and laughter as being release feelings. Our bodies may need to release pent up experiences that have become locked into our cellular structure. Expressing these feelings in a safe place can be very healing. They do not need to be expressed to those involved in the provocation of our feelings.

Unfortunately from a Gestalt point of view, many spiritual and psychological approaches, as well as parenting ones, offer techniques to help us diminish our feelings—or literally bypass them. Many of these techniques were taught to us as children, particularly boys who were taught not to cry or be scared. Labels, such as cry baby, sissy, scaredy cat were devastating for children. Such methods lead to diminished feelings, and unfortunately they also promote superficiality, being out of touch, and being inauthentic.

In Gestalt we accept deep feelings as part of our aliveness. Feeling deeply allows us to experience others and ourselves more fully. It informs us of our world and those in it beyond a superficial level. Our deep feelings are felt in every cell in our bodies, which become cleansed through experiencing them. It is part of our human nature, not a sign that something is wrong with us that we need to "get over". These feelings include passion, grief, love, rage, hurt, disgust, joy, contentment, shame, and fear. When we express them we may experience new insights that help us mature and move along on our journey of life.

The Buddhists encourage us to feel our feelings. They say that suffering is the human condition, and that growing and learning is a result of acknowledging our feelings and suffering.

Loss of a loved one is often the catalyst to feeling deeply. Elizabeth Kubler Ross developed a model to help us deal with loss. She talks about the feelings of disbelief, fear, anger, numbness and grief as part of the process most of us go through.

Then there are a whole lot of other feelings called our neurotic feelings. These are jealousy, envy, guilt, embarrassment, self-consciousness, feeling silly, and feeling stupid. These feelings are worth some therapy sessions to lessen their impact on us, but mostly these have to do with our expectations of ourselves and others. They are very important to explore, as it is these feelings that often stop us from developing ourselves more fully.

Learning to accept or embrace "what is", and the deep feelings that are evoked, is key to our growth according to Buddhists, Ekhart Tolle, Gestalt therapists, and others. The acceptance of "what is" allows us to move on. In this way we are not fighting our truth, which takes up a lot of energy and keeps us stuck, often in neurotic anxiety and depression.

ALIVENESS

Gestalt people are in the business of teaching us how to be more of who we are. This includes feeling more, experiencing more poignant moments, having more moments of synchronicity, allowing for more spiritual and intuitive moments, and experiencing deeper contact. For many years I've referred colleagues, friends and clients to a poem written by Oriah Mountain Dreamer called the Invitation. She depicts so beautifully the passion that is important in her life.

You can read her poem on line at www.oriahmountaindreamer.com .

EXPERIMENTS

1. *Which deep feelings do you avoid FEELING? Which ones do you allow? Do you avoid feeling anger, sadness or fear?*

2. *Which feelings do you avoid EXPRESSING?*

3. *How do you stop yourself from feeling anger, grief, fear?*

4. *Which of the neurotic feelings do you struggle with? How do they get in your way?*

We acknowledge here that it is not only important to feel our feelings, but to understand where they come from as well. Often our thinking and expectations can cause certain emotional reactions, and once we change our thinking patterns, our feelings change. Also, sometimes our feelings are the result of thinking in generalities, rather than specifics. Once we face the details our feelings may change. These more specific aspects of our emotional life are best dealt with in therapy, Gestalt therapy, if possible, as Gestalt therapists are usually specifically trained to handle deep emotions, including anger and rage. Many therapists who have not dealt with their own deep feelings, may be afraid of yours.

3. VULNERABILITY

"Openness doesn't come from resisting our fears, but from getting to know them well." Pema Chodron, Comfortable with Uncertainty

Not only are we physically vulnerable, but emotionally and spiritually as well. The sad thing is that we are encouraged to cover up our vulnerability, even hide it from ourselves… or spend a lot of money 'trying' to make it go away.

Social work professor, Brené Brown presented a 20 minute delightful and funny talk for TED, called *The Power of Vulnerability*. She does a magnificent job of showing how hard it has been for her to even know she feels vulnerable, much less acknowledge it. Check out her talk online at: www.ted.com/talks/brene_brown_on_vulnerability.html.

Why is this important? We Gestalt people are in the business of encouraging us to know ourselves better, and to tell ourselves our truth. However, being human, many of us might prefer to forget a lot about ourselves, including our vulnerabilities.

As we get older and begin to have issues with our bodies changing, such as our ability to move fast, we probably feel vulnerable more frequently. At a local nursing home an elderly client of mine who is wheel chair bound, told me he was scared of a large man who had dementia and no impulse control. Unlike many other residents, this man told me loud and clear that he felt vulnerable. I was impressed at his ability to be so open and direct about his fears. He is an exception, I'm sure.

Can you imagine yourself saying
- I am scared
- I feel shaky
- I feel vulnerable

Acknowledging our truth, to ourselves and others, demonstrates our openness and acceptance of who we are. (See Chapter B2: *Telling Ourselves the Truth*.)

EXPERIMENT

1. *Tell someone close to you that you feel vulnerable at times, and notice the effects on that person.*

2. *Many will move into fix-it mode and try to "make you feel better." Invite them to accept your vulnerability, as you have. It is part of being human, you can tell them. Now ask them if they ever feel vulnerable.*

4. BEING DIRECT

"What is said is to be taken literally." – Premises of Navaho Life & Thought, Clyde Kluckholm, Navaho

BEING DIRECT VERSUS BEING INDIRECT

Learning *how* to be clear and direct with others (and ourselves) is a big part of Gestalt teachings. This in no way implies that you *should* be direct all the time. Being aware, knowing how and having the choice are what counts.

Becoming aware of how we are being indirect is essential to understand being direct. This can be a fun exploration. It is amazing how circumspect we can be.

QUALIFYING

Qualifying what we are saying protects us from having to make a clear stand. "Well I sort of would like to go to the movies, though perhaps at another time, if…" You get the picture. This person may have been taught not to offend anyone, and thus has trouble saying "No, I don't want to go to the movies. Is there something else we can do that we can agree to?"

One strange type of qualification happened when I was in my 20s and lived in a remote Mexican village for 2 months with the American Friends Service Committee, helping the villagers build school benches, among other things. This program was like a mini-Peace Corp connected to the Quakers. I will never forget, after learning a little bit of "village Spanish", asking a young man if he wanted us to pick some plums for him on our walk back from a nearby village. His answer was no, but in his culture it wasn't polite to say so. Instead he said "Si" and shook his finger left and right to indicate the "no". Needless to say we were a little confused as to which of the two opposite messages to believe until someone showed us the "yes", which simply was "Si" without the hand movement.

SPEAKING IN GENERALITIES, or NOT RESPONDING

There are many other ways to be indirect, as you well know. Speaking generally rather than specifically is another one. "Would you like to go to the movies tonight?" she asked. "Movies aren't what they used to be. Remember when… ", etc. This person never did respond to the request.

NUMEROUS OTHER INDIRECT WAYS

Giving double messages is another way of being indirect, as in the Mexican scene above. Telling someone you are angry with them while you are smiling is another common one. Certain gestures can minimize our directness. Ending our sentences at a higher pitch makes it sound like a question rather than a statement, thus minimizing our directness. Often when people minimize their statements in one of these ways, they sound like they don't mean what they say. I realize that I often don't take them very seriously. When I tell them this, they are surprised, and usually work hard to be more direct, as they often have felt that no one hears them or is interested in them.

IT IS YOUR CHOICE TO BE DIRECT OR NOT

This doesn't mean you *"should"* always be clear and direct. This is your choice. Remember that *"through awareness comes choice"*. There have been many times when a clerk in a store asks me "Do you have anything planned for the day" and when one person saw the shocked look on my face, she changed it to "Do you have anything fun planned for the day?" I chose to go along with this game and said yes, I was going to the movies later on. My outrageous self wanted to say "No, I'm in a very bad mood today and don't want to be around anyone." Obviously she had no intention of my being clear and direct with her.

But with those we are close to, knowing *how* to be clear and direct can make relationships more functional, as long as your partner wants to do so, too. Then you can avoid the manipulations, second guessing, and other games we all play when we are too afraid to be direct. And even then there will be times when you don't want to be direct. Learning *how* to be direct gives you a choice.

BEING DIRECT WITHOUT OUR JUDGMENTAL LABELS

Being direct does not mean sharing our judgmental labels with one another such as "That was stupid," or "When are you going to grow up?".

With those close to us, learning to be direct without judging, and taking responsibility for our thoughts and feelings can enhance our relationships. "I get upset and uncomfortable when you get loud and mad at our kids. Can we talk about it as I'm not sure how I might need to change, and I want to hear how you might be willing to change." In this example, the person took responsibility by saying in effect: "I get upset, when you yell at the kids and I'm open to looking at what this is about for me."

EXPERIMENTS

1. *Watch people in restaurants, in parks, wherever you can hear them, and listen for their qualifiers.*

2. *Listen for your own. Exaggerate using qualifiers with good friends. See if they notice. Then experiment with not using them.*

3. *What other ways do you use to be indirect? Exaggerate these, which will help you become more aware of doing this..*

4. *Now be direct and clear without judging.*

5. CONTACT, WITHDRAWAL

"There is always a cycle of interdependency between the organism and the environment." – Fritz Perls, Ego, Hunger and Aggression

OUR NATURAL RHYTHM

Healthy children if allowed to come and go according to their desires might have a sense of their natural rhythm. They would eat when hungry, sleep when tired, make contact whenever and retreat when they felt the need for it. We are constantly moving towards connecting and moving away to reflect and regroup.

OUR NATURAL RHYTHM GETS DISTORTED AND BLOCKED

Of course many are not able to do this easily due to the busy lives we create for ourselves. In addition the culture demands much of us which may not be congruent with our rhythm.

In the USA during the last 60 years, alone time has not been valued by our culture. Keeping constantly active and busy, is valued. So many of us push ourselves, never allowing for a time out, a different point of view, new scenery, or even a vacation. I recall years ago when the doctor told my workaholic parents to park their kids with friends and take a month off. They did, and went to a ranch in Montana. It did wonders for them.

Even on the Navajo Reservation where I worked for some years, I found that children are encouraged to get up very early, put their shoes on immediately, and keep busy (go to school, sometimes 2-3 hours away, do homework, tend sheep, take care of Grandma and other chores), until they go to bed at night, meaning they could finally take off their shoes. The message was, don't stop.

On a few occasions I referred clients to a travel agent, telling them, "you don't need therapy now, you need a vacation!".

THE WAVE

Fritz Perls once described the contact-withdrawal dynamic as being like a wave: it flows into the shore making contact, then recedes to replenish itself; then it flows into the shore and recedes again, and again, and again. It has a rhythm to it. We have the need to flow back and forth as we go through our days making contact with others and our environment and then withdrawing to integrate and digest our experiences. This dynamic is relaxed and natural if we have developed it according to our own rhythm.

However many of us have not found a natural way to come and go. We've had a history of being on someone else's timetable: our parents', the school system's, etc. So we often are not flowing, but rather tensing, not breathing fully, making poor contact or none at all and not getting revitalized during the withdrawal time. Many of us are conflicted about taking time to pull away as it isn't polite, or we tell ourselves that we *should* be there all the time. So our withdrawal time is fraught with inner conflict. And this can affect our physical, mental and spiritual health over time.

How wonderful it would be if we and our loved ones could follow our natural rhythms. And wouldn't it be wonderful if no one got upset if someone told them directly "I need to be alone now." Life would be so much more relaxed and comfortable. Of course this isn't realistic in many situations, such as with our boss, our friends, or relatives.

And, once couples and partners are more in touch with their rhythms they may not coincide with one another's. This then, may require special adaptation especially when a gregarious organizer extrovert falls in love with a Buddhist writer introvert. Good luck! It can be done when each honors the others' need to contact and withdraw in their own way.

BLOCKING

Blocking occurs when we can't or won't be ourselves when we are with others. Many people put themselves through all kinds of contortions with this issue. They have difficulty saying no, or saying they want to stop now. They may try to give indirect messages through body language, telling white lies or being manipulative: "*You* look tired; I think we should go home now." I recently heard on the news that people will use their iPod as an excuse to withdraw. This way they don't have to be direct or make meaningful connections with others.

If we were not allowed to follow our own rhythm because of the *shoulds* of childhood, we may have developed behaviors to protect ourselves. For example, we may have tensed every time our mother said "look at me when I'm talking", or slightly turned our back towards someone we don't want to be with at that moment, causing chronic cramping in our bodies.

After many years of being the good girl I realized how afraid I was of being asked some questions, as I felt I *should* answer *all* of them. And answer them honestly. I was really boxed in. What power that gives other people, and how powerless I was. I became hyper-alert at times and would be sure to have an exit plan if I sensed someone might ask me something I didn't want to answer. I developed ways to weasel out of answering questions in one dysfunctional way or another: such as changing the subject, answering some other question, asking the person why they wanted to know, making up an excuse to leave, or pretending I hadn't heard them. I'm sure I contorted my body to give a message to stay away from asking me any questions.

My life changed when I realized I didn't have to answer every question someone asked me! I luckily learned to tell the truth; I learned to say I didn't want to answer their question, in a nice way, of course. This freed me and allowed me to be more comfortable connecting with others. My rhythm of contact and withdrawal changed.

Then I have fun with this at times, as I believe that asking questions can be intrusive. Try answering the grocery store clerk when she asks you "how is your day going so far" with "I'd rather not talk about it." I then tell them to share with their human relations department that their questions can be offensive and intrusive to some of us. Others like to be asked.

There is a true story about an Anglo (white) person who, in typical fashion, asked a Native American friend of hers "How are you?" The Native American did not respond. This confused the Anglo woman, as she was used to everyone answering her. She didn't say anything to the woman for fear of making a cultural blunder. A week later the Native

American friend came up to her and said, "I've been thinking about what you asked me last week…"

How comfortable are you reaching out to others when you want to connect and then how comfortable are you at retreating when you're ready to move on?

EXPERIMENTS

1. *Do you have a sense of your own rhythm of coming and going, of contact and withdrawal?*

2. *Notice how you don't follow your own rhythm in certain situations but not in other situations. For example, maybe you are good at telling your children when you need a time out, but not your spouse.*

3. *Get to know how you deal with not following your own natural rhythm. Notice if you tense, hold your breath, and/or contort your physical body. Notice how this behavior affects you mentally and emotionally as well.*

4. *Allow your own natural rhythm even at the risk of upsetting someone. For example, tell your friend or partner when you need to withdraw.*

5. *Do you ever force yourself to be in contact with some one longer than you want because you are afraid to be alone in that moment?*

6. CONGRUENCE

"I want to turn paper people into real people." – Fritz Perls

Being authentic isn't easy after years of playing games with ourselves and others to get what we want, particularly if our games work, at least some of the time! Playing the game of the "charmer" who makes women feel good, is a hard one to give up. After learning to be responsible for all the hearts he broke, and the children he fathered in the process, the charmer may be glad to give up this role. Playing the game of the caretaker may be hard to give up as it makes the woman feel good. However, after awhile she may get burned out and then sees the game she has been playing. Then she wants out.

Being "congruent" means being centered and authentic. It means that my words, my body language, my actions and my tone of voice all say the same thing. Incongruence is when we give the mixed messages, often without being aware. "I wouldn't be here if I didn't love you," he said in an annoyed voice when she questioned his love." "Of course I love you," the irritated mother said to her son. "Yes, I'm upset with you," she said as she giggled.

A lot of the Gestalt work is attending to incongruence since it is so prevalent and so obvious to those trained to *see* and *hear* clearly in the present. How we dress and present ourselves, is part of this message as well. I found the following quote about a Navajo response to Anglo tourists visiting the Navajo reservation.

"They wondered why these people were so eager to wear clothing that made them look foolish. Navajos saw balding men as those who usually did not have sense enough to wear hats and who wore strange looking short pants that revealed even stranger looking legs. They shook their heads at the sight of older women with unnatural hair colors who tried but failed to look like much younger women. These white people had time but they always seemed to be in a hurry; they had money and privilege yet they rarely seemed to be happy." – Peter Iverson, DINE: A History of the Navajos 2002

Indigenous groups take congruence a big step further. For example the Navajos encourage us to be in balance and harmony with Mother Earth and Father Sky. They first have to be congruent with themselves. Then they need to work to be in harmony and balance with that which is greater than themselves. This focus allows them to attend to all beings and all of nature in their ceremonies and prayers.

While working on the Navajo Reservation for 10 years, I became involved with a wonderful organization called Adopt-a-Native-Elder. I've kept in touch with the elder I adopted. She speaks no English, but her adult son translates for me when I visit or write her. As a sheep herder, she would say the Beauty Way prayer over and over again while tending sheep. In English it goes something like this:

Beauty* Way Prayer
(*beauty here means harmony and balance)

There is beauty before me
There is beauty behind me
There is beauty above me
There is beauty below me
There is beauty all around me

She took this prayer very seriously and said it all the time according to her son. It kept her in harmony and balance with Mother Earth and Father Sky and with everyone around her. I could see from the way she was and the sparkle in her eyes, that this prayer indeed, kept her aligned with herself and the universe.

EXPERIMENTS

1. *Watch people you interact with regularly and observe how congruent they are. Notice their voices, body language and breathing if you can. Are their words saying the same thing as the rest of them.*

2. *Now, watch yourself in a similar way. Are you congruent. When aren't you? Because we have blind spots, see if a friend or partner can give you feedback about this.*

3. *If you are incongruent at times, experiment with being congruent. How does that feel?*

Section E

THE MAGIC AND SACRED IN GESTALT*

1. **Slow Down; You Move too Fast**

2. **Being Present**

3. **Making Contact**

4. **Being Open to the Unexpected**

5. **The Magic and Sacred in Gestalt**

*If you feel challenged doing the experiments in this section of the book, please read the chapter in **Section F: How All of These Practices Relate to Gestalt Therapy.**

Slow down, you move too fast.

1. SLOW DOWN; YOU MOVE TOO FAST*

Answer the phone; text your friend; read the news on the internet; rush to your office; grab a cup of coffee... Are you breathing? Are you aware of the smelly perfume on the lady standing next to you? Can you see the sky clouding over? Can you hear the sirens nearby? Are you aware of your senses?

For years Gestalt people have been teaching their students and clients how to slow down and experience their worlds. And that was before computers, cell phones, texting and the like! We've gotten more distracted and more in a hurry. God help us! Seriously.

We have this incredible body which is extremely intricate in its creation. It can do a lot of things and it can experience even more. We underestimate ourselves. By slowing down we can experience not only our senses but the subtle inner awarenesses, the subtle sensations, the sounds of silence and myriad other phenomena.

It is like the story of the Tortoise and the Hare. Hare, arrogant and cocky, rushes past Tortoise smirking. Tortoise is ambling along smelling everything in sight... going slowly and enjoying his journey. While Hare is looking the other way, distracted, Tortoise crosses the finish line first.

Yes, there is a time to go fast, to get things done. But we've trained ourselves to live in the "fast lane" and it is hard to break out of it, even for a short time now and then. So now people have to go to meditation retreats to slow down. Many have trouble quieting their minds, so they go to another retreat and then another. I wonder if they ever teach themselves to slow down in their daily lives from moment to moment.. Take a breath; pause; look around; and of course smell the roses, or watch the sadness on the faces of their struggling friends and neighbors. Or notice their own sadness, which is trying to break through. Slowing down gives us time to be more authentic and alive in every way.

*The title of a song by Simon and Garfunkel

EXPERIMENT

1. *With awareness, do everything very fast. Exaggerate this. Talk fast, move fast, breathe fast, read fast, text fast. Now do it even faster. Then stop and see how you feel.*

2. *Now take a few slow deep breaths. And with awareness, do everything more slowly. Exaggerate this. Talk slower, move slower, read slower, text slower, breathe slower. Stop and see what you experience.*

3. *What did you miss when you went fast?*

4. *Take some time, such as a half hour, every so often and be like the Tortoise, moving slowly, savoring each moment. And always pay attention to how you feel during and after.*

2. BEING PRESENT

"Silence is a potent carrier of presence,
so be aware of the silence
between & underneath the words.
Be aware of the gaps.
To listen to the silence, wherever you are,
is an easy and direct way of becoming present.
Nothing truly new and creative can come
into this world except through the gaps,
that clear space of infinite possibility."

– Eckhart Tolle, The Power of Now

In an earlier chapter, I described the three zones of awareness: inner, outer, middle. *Being present* involves the inner and outer zones in particular, in which you are exquisitely aware of what your senses are picking up in the environment and of your inner response to all of this. Your middle zone thinking is at a minimum, but your mind's intuitive and creative functions are wide open to whatever appears.

In this state you are most likely

- Congruent and authentic
- Seeing specifically and concretely what is
- Seeing the bigger picture as you take in the background
- Feeling alive and curious
- Hearing what is actually said, as well as meta messages such as noticing body language (without making interpretations)
- Savoring and experiencing fully
- Comfortable in silence
- Allowing whatever emerges in you and the other

- Open to the unexpected
- Respecting your contact withdrawal rhythm and that of others
- Unaffected by distractions such as thinking, unfinished business.

Learning to be present in the here and now is one of the most important Gestalt teachings.

- It is where we can experience ourselves most fully. It is where our soul lives.
- It is the road to our unconscious, to those aspects of ourselves that we have hidden and need attention.
- It is where our intuition and creativity live.
- It is where we can experience our relationship to that which is greater than we are.
- It is from this place that we can make deep meaningful contact with others, as we slow down enough to be able to experience another's eyes, to see into their soul. We are open, congruent, in harmony and balance. We are alive.
- It can be a place of deep healing. If you are a therapist or counselor, put aside your theories about diagnosis, crisis intervention, trouble shooting, consulting, and advising. Just be present with your client with no agenda or plan and see what unfolds.

Psychic Healer, Inelia, from Peru is interviewed about this very topic. Inelia said about what she does:

"The best way to describe it would be that my focus goes (to the patient). And I am there 110 percent in every dimension, in every time-space for that moment… I don't do anything, I don't have any intention. I don't have any attachment to outcome. I don't have any curiosity. Nothing. It's just complete focus. And what appears to happen is, then there's something else—whatever it is, the Divine force, energy, chi, whatever—comes through."

Inelia mentions she has no attachment to outcome. She does not have any intention. This means she doesn't set any goals for the client. Her left brain is on vacation. So she is totally open to whatever happens. She is just *present* in that moment as fully as she knows how to be. This is what we teach therapists to be able to do. This is what we teach everyone to be able to do.

This in no way means we *should* always follow this approach! It is very different from many of the healing modalities where the therapist or the healer has an intention for the client to heal or a goal to achieve. Having goals and agendas are very important for many things in our life. We have a left brain and we need to use it. Some believe this helps to direct us.

However, *being present* as I've described here, is done without an agenda or goal. From this place something unexpected may happen, whether it be a healing or a new awareness. This is what happens to many who experience the Gestalt therapist's presence with them. Often they experience what they call magic in these moments. From Inelia's description above, it sounds plausible.

EXPERIMENT
Sit with a friend or partner in silence for 3 minutes or so. Be as present as you can. With an open heart, observe, sense, see and hear fully who is before you. Experience her fully. Share your experience without judging and analyzing after the 3 minutes.

3. MAKING CONTACT

"'Who ARE you?' said the Caterpillar to Alice." – Lewis Carroll, Alice in Wonderland

In order to make meaningful contact we have to be open to the understanding that all human beings are unique and have a soul or spirit with which we can connect. Deep connections occur between these aspects of ourselves. The same is true with animals, particularly those we have as pets. If we believe others are less than us, and "thing-a-fy" them, as Fritz used to say, we see them as objects, thus we are not open to their mystery, making deep contact impossible.

About 10 years ago my cat, Soxy, was dying. I laid on the bed with her and we looked into one another's eyes for 45 minutes. I felt a very powerful and loving connection with her, and then she left. It was a very moving experience for me, and I imagine it was for her, too. This was one of a number of memorable moments in my life. If Fritz had been there he might have said, "Ah ha! You just had a mini-satori," Fritz' shorthand for a peak experience.

Hopefully, we've all had moments in our lives where we have felt a spark of connectedness when experiencing another person or animal. It is often these moments that we treasure the most. Learning to be *fully present* is essential and the more we practice being present the easier it gets and the more often it happens. (See Chapter E2: *Being Present*.)

Contact is not always fun and joyful, as we all know, but it is usually meaningful. We can connect with our anger, our pain and sadness, and our vulnerability. We begin to experience the essence of the other, and not just the outward aspects of their form and behavior. To do this we have to really pay attention to ourselves and the other, without blocking our aliveness, even if someone is angry with us.

I recently heard an aide in a nursing home say to an elder expressing her anger in German, "Please get angry at me in English so I can understand why you are angry with me." Good for her! She wanted to know! She wanted to connect with the elder, and she was open to receiving feedback.

RELATIONSHIPS & COMMUNITY

These connecting moments are meaningful and essential to our aliveness. As herd animals we want to be in community, close to one another, rather than isolated and alone in the world, an unnatural condition modern society has evolved in to. So often these moments ring out as hope, as an omen.

In a healthy community, these moments of contact happen frequently with many people. Recently I saw my neighbors whom I hadn't seen in a few months. While talking with them for awhile, I felt their openness and beauty in a way I hadn't before. I felt nourished just being in their presence. I've no idea if they had changed, if I had changed or if there was something in the air. It didn't matter. I was deeply touched being with them.

CONTACT IS THE APPRECIATION OF DIFFERENTNESS

When we attend to one another fully, some people become uncomfortable, as they are not used to being seen or heard. They may have a life time of protecting others from knowing them. Or some don't see and hear fully, but only experience others as labels. Slowly good genuine contact can dissolve these boundaries.

And sometimes people are not used to letting themselves see differences in one another. A couple I asked to do this many years ago felt anxious. The wife said "I don't know if I want to know you better as I may see some differences, and that might mean we should break up." This is the cause-effect thinking mentioned in the first chapter.

We teach people to see differences and to put themselves in others' shoes. Much of the role playing in Gestalt allows us to experience being others in their worlds. Although many believe we can't really do it, you'd be surprised at how accurate we are able to role play others, which the "others" often validate. This rich experimentation broadens our awareness of what it is like to be someone else and how rich a relationship can be if two people are different. Try the fun and often funny experiments that follow!

HOW AND WHEN WE STOP OURSELVES FROM CONTACT

To reiterate from earlier chapters the egalitarian contactful way of life is one many of us have never been taught to do very successfully. Most often we relate as either the topdog or underdog, the parent or the child, the teacher or the student, the boss or the employee, the master or the slave—or a number of other roles, which are only a small part of who we are. A lot of our postures and gestures reveal these dysfunctional roles, often in the form of physical blocks such as tight chests, superficial breathing, ticks, furrowed brows, and the like, which cover our deep desire to be loved and respected as equals. How seldom you hear, "He (or she) really sees who I am!"

Many of us don't want to be seen. We are ashamed of our lives and ourselves. We may have had unhappy experiences of abandonment, betrayal or abuse, and thus we have created numerous ways to protect ourselves from further hurt, blocking these possible connecting moments. Or we may have been perpetrators. (See Chapter B3&4: *How We Protect Ourselves with our Postures, Gestures, and Voice*; and *How We Protect Ourselves With the Games We Play*.)

The modern day communities in the USA don't protect and take care of its members as they did years ago, thus modern man and woman have withdrawn into themselves, protecting themselves as best they can. Because our society is so mobile, we often don't live in one place long enough to create strong bonds with others. And in marriages or relationships, each come with their own histories of family values and structure as well as personal trauma. It is hard to establish a feeling of trust and safety since there are no culturally agreed upon expectations and assumptions anymore. Each couple has to consciously create a family structure they can both count on, a daunting task without guidelines! Those who are part of the same religious or cultural community often have an easier time than others with this structure. Once the members feel a sense of shared expectations and assumptions, they are more likely to be open and able to connect deeply with one another.

EXPERIMENTS

1. *How do you stop yourself from being open for deep contact?*

2. *Ask a friend or partner "What is it like to be you when you...". (Pick a theme such as when you first get up in the morning, realize you are late for an appointment, discover someone is angry with you, etc). This way you are showing great interest in this person and how she might be similar or different than you.*

3. *Set up two chairs. Role play a person important to you, discussing a mutual concern. Now role play yourself responding. Dialogue back and forth, changing chairs. What it was like to play the other person. Did you learn anything new about him or her? About yourself?*

Open to the unexpected.

4. BEING OPEN TO THE UNEXPECTED

"To be fully alive, fully human and completely awake is to be continually thrown out of the nest." – Pema Chodron, Buddhist Teacher & Author

Most of us were raised to set goals, plan ahead, and work towards these goals. Our left brain is in gear and the road we choose will hopefully lead to success, whatever that might be. For many since WWII until the early 2000s we planned our education, our careers, or financial capabilities, where we wanted to live, expecting our lives would unfold as planned.

As we all know, that is not what is happening now in 2012. We have quickly gone from a somewhat predictable life to one that is unknown. We are living in a time of uncertainty with the health of the planet, job possibilities, education, affordability. Everything is up in the air. Pema Chodron in the quote above assures us that to be fully alive and awake we need to be thrown out of the nest. Well, that is happening to most of us now. So, now what do we do, you ask!

Gestalt practices teach us to learn how to ride the waves of change by being open to the unexpected. This could mean giving up identifying with a particular career or life style. If things really change in our world, we might not be rich anymore, or famous, or powerful. We might just be a human being without any accoutrements. Or the opposite could happen.

At one of the first two week long Gestalt workshops I attended, all participants were asked to not reveal anything about their life styles or careers. Rather than using our names, the group came up with a name to call each of us. For two weeks we had to rely on being seen for who we were in the present. This was quite a difficult experience for many, as you can imagine. How do you do that, you ask!

Here is where we invite people to go inside themselves, to listen to their inner knowing. Most of our education did not fund right brain intuitive learning so we aren't familiar with listening to our creative unconscious. So hopefully these practices will help you do this inner exploring. This is where we should be living more of the time. This is where we will find where our feet are taking us now.

As we explore we may find a lot of unfinished business we haven't dealt with, which keeps popping up whenever we are open and looking within. Many of the practices in this book might shed some light on your issues.

There is a wonderful children's book called *There is a Nightmare in My Closet*, by Mercer Mayer that I see as a Gestalt children's book. It is about a 4 year old terrified little boy, who confronts the blob (the nightmare) that comes out of his closet. The dialogue they have is priceless and unexpected, which often happens when we deal directly with people and life. He shoots the nightmare with his toy gun, which causes the nightmare to cry. The little boy then tells it to be quiet so it doesn't wake his parents. And then he invites the nightmare into bed with him and consoles him. Now who would have expected that as an outcome? You never know. So staying open to the unexpected might bring forth the unimaginable. Are you game?

It is time to put to rest for awhile the robotic left brain training that taught us to compartmentalize, give up our values and not be in touch with life, and only achievement instead.

We are interested in getting below logical thinking and planning, and get to the creative unconscious. By being open to the unexpected, we make a space for our creativity and inner knowing to emerge, or perhaps we'll experience others more fully as we see and hear them. In this space, too, we might see unconscious and unfinished conflicts and pain we haven't dealt with yet. All of these are important to come forth. They are part of our deeper being, which has probably been ignored for far too long.

EXPERIMENTS

1. *Create a special box in your imagination and put it beside you on the floor. Fill it with all your labels, concepts, evaluations, judgments, and theories for now. You can have them back later whenever you want them.. Just do so with awareness!*

2. *Then sit quietly and see what emerges on its own without your controlling it. If something upsetting emerges, don't run away from it. Accept it, without over analyzing it. If nothing emerges, sit with the silence and nothingness. Accept whatever happens. If a concept or judgment slips into your awareness, imagine dropping it into your box. And then continue to see what emerges without all of your mind's productions.*

As noted above, the world has changed a lot in the last few years and more and more we are living with uncertainty. It is not possible to plan for the future anymore. We don't know what will happen to the economy, to our social institutions such as our schools, our work places. Everything is open-ended now. We need to develop flexibility muscles. As many of my Navajo friends used to say, that because of the horrific experiences of their ancestors they learned to be "adaptable", and now they pride themselves for finding this way to handle whatever comes into their world.

The more we can learn to be open to the unexpected, and ride the waves of uncertainty, both inside ourselves and in our lives, the better off we will be. As some say, "Get used to it!" Pema Chodron in the quote above reminds us of the importance of being thrown out of the nest, again and again.

5. THE MAGIC AND SACRED IN GESTALT: The Creative Void

"Out beyond the ideas of right and wrong doing there is a field.
I will meet you there." – Rumi

"All the things that truly matter—beauty, love, creativity, joy,
inner peace—arise from beyond the mind," – Eckhart Tolle,
The Power of Now.

CREATIVITY AND SPIRITUALITY

Fritz often referenced a place he called the void, the fertile void or the creative void. Creativity was key in his lexicon, acknowledging a special kind of awareness. Since he never used the word spiritual, many of his students, like myself, felt Fritz' use of the word creativity covered what many of us refer to as spiritual now.

Not long ago I spoke with someone who trained with Lore Perls in New York for many years as well as with Fritz before he moved to the West Coast. He said they stayed away from the word "spiritual" because Hitler, whom they escaped from in 1933, was obsessed with the occult. He and Lore studied Zen in Germany in the 1920s I understand, and later in life Fritz went to Asia to broaden his awareness of Buddhist teachings.

To use Fritz's language, the Creative or Fertile Void can be likened to the quiet moment, the gap, that both Pema Chodron, Buddhist teacher, and Eckhard Tolle refer to often. If you are paying attention and slowed down you can find it at the end of each sentence, between words, at the end of each breath, or when you are fully present. It is here where inspiration emerges, where the direction of our lives can become clear, and where profound understandings occur. During these moments we are most likely to be in the here and now, slowed down and in a quiet space.

Back in the late 1980s I facilitated a weekend workshop in Mendocino County. During a break I took a walk and found a bench overlooking rolling California hills with the occasional life oak tree dotting the landscape. It was very quiet as I sat there for a few minutes. Suddenly and totally unexpected, I saw, inside myself, a banner flying by me slowly with the words *California is no longer your home* on it. I sobbed for some time, not because I didn't want to leave the state, but because I knew deep inside that it was the truth. I was aligned at that moment. A very clear message came to me in the *gap*, the stillness, the void.

NAVAJO WAY OF LIFE

Soon after returning home to the Bay Area I put my house on the market and within 6 months moved to Sedona, Arizona. This was no cosmic accident, as in Arizona I worked part time on the Navajo Nation, running wellness programs, and working with the medicine men and women. I discovered that many Native Americans honor being aligned with the universal forces as well as aligned with one's self. The Navajos call this *Hozho*. And their Beauty Way Ceremony honors this harmony and balance.

Navajo medicine people are trained in their early years, not attending regular schools until they are older. These children, with the help of their elder spiritual teachers, can tune into many dimensions of existence and into their special abilities to see and hear beyond the reality to which we are accustomed. It is from this place that they develop their healing abilities.

A medicine man I knew well told me that his parents hid him when he was young so that the government authorities wouldn't abduct him and put him in a boarding school far from his home and family, as they did to most Indian children until the 1950s. At 12 he finally went to first grade in a California boarding school after he had developed his intuitive abilities to make him eligible to be a medicine man. If he had gone to school when he was 5 and learned how to read and write as was required by his teachers, he would not have developed his inner knowing at a young age.

Another man, a Navajo social worker, whom I know recalls that his parents told him he would make a good medicine man, but since he was taken from his home at 5 and put into a boarding school, he did not develop the necessary abilities at the right age to be one. After many years of schooling he got a master's degree in social work, the next best thing to being a medicine man, he felt.

Two school teachers on the Navajo Nation, one Anglo (white), the other Navajo, decided to start a school for children that would not restrict their intuitive development. As far as I know the school never got off the ground as the Navajo teacher died. Some believe it was witchcraft that did her in. Both felt that the required teachings in the early grades prevent children from developing their inner guidance and they wanted their school to honor this development by changing the focus of their teachings.

All of these stories honor the importance of knowing ourself as well as developing our intuitive abilities. The Navajos, whom I know better than other indigenous groups, encouraged this development for everyone, not just medicine people. Their ceremonies, including the Peyote ceremonies of the Native American Church, invited participants to know themselves on many levels. On occasion I met someone on the reservation whom I knew was highly developed spiritually. They had a calmness and knowingness about them and an indescribable look in their eyes that felt different, almost other worldly. I was deeply touched every time I was in the presence of one of these people.

After 10 years of working at a clinic on Navajo, I became aware that their "way of life" had some things in common with the Gestalt way of life. The key, of course, is awareness and the development of their creativity and intuition.

LANGUAGE

Our language, English, being less specific and concrete than the Navajo language, allows us to be vague. Fritz often encouraged us to be more descriptive of our experiences and to get away from generalities and concepts as much as possible. He felt experiencing the descriptive details gets us and our listeners closer to our experience. The Navajos do this with their concrete and specific language. They are finely tuned to listening, seeing and experiencing their world. They don't miss a trick! Many of their jokes are about the details of what they see and hear. Our language is often unclear and vague to them, and their jokes reflect this. A Medicine Man friend laughs when he asks me if anyone has "kicked the bucket" lately. Like in his own language he took this literally, and he couldn't understand why this meant someone had died.

Another aspect of Navajo language is that they have many verbs. Since life is constantly in motion, verbs reflect this. They are words about movement. Nouns are concepts that put parameters around the subject matter, making things looked fixed and rigid or not moving in the natural flow of life. So if I identify with the noun *happiness*, I may not make any room for other experiences in my life. I might try to defy the natural order and convince myself I am happy, when I am not some of the time. If asked what one wants most in life a white person might say he wants to be happy, whereas a traditional Navajo might say they want to be in balance and harmony with the natural order of the universe.

SUBTLE ENERGIES AND INNER KNOWING

Fritz encouraged us to be more attuned to the subtleties and specifics of our experiences. For example, Navajo elders, by shaking our hand softly, can tune into us. From their awareness they are in contact with the subtle energies of the universe whether these have to do with a person's health (harmony and balance), or with the energies of the grandmothers and grandfathers whom they say visit from other realms. By shaking our hands in this way, it is as if gentle contact with our pulses informs them of who we are.

Many people who meditate attain this harmony and balance, and healthy young children do as well. Elders are likely to have reached this state more often than when they were younger. It is those in their middle years who are too busy dealing with the ups and downs of life that have the most difficulty attaining this balance.

Interestingly at age 26, when I first met Fritz, I felt a strange sense come over me. He was leading a Gestalt Dream Workshop in Berkeley, California in 1961. I sat quietly watching him work with someone, and suddenly the following thought came to me, totally out of the blue, "I am going to be doing this work for the rest of my life." And here, 50 years later, I am doing just that and have been since that time. If I hadn't been in a quiet and reflective state, I might have missed this message.

Many Gestalt people have fine-tuned and expanded their consciousness through all of the awareness experiences they've had both teaching and doing Gestalt therapy over the years. They can tune into some of the same energies as do many indigenous peoples not only in their daily lives, but when they are working with clients. I've heard some Gestalt therapists say, myself included, "Some of the time I'm in an altered state when I work." What is this state? I see it as being fully present in myself and with my client. We both are open to what will emerge in the here and now. We are aligned and in balance. This space, the Creative Void, feels Sacred. It feels like magic. And here magic often happens.

These practices, which can expand our awareness, our aliveness, our creativity and our ability to connect with ourselves and others in deep and meaningful ways. These are for anyone who is curious, as well as for trainees and clients in Gestalt therapy. It is these teachings that I refer to as the Gestalt Way of Life.

EXPERIMENT

Review your life and recall a special moment when you were inspired, or had a profound, out of the ordinary or spiritual experience. If you like, do this again, and again. Share them with a friend and invite your friend to share a special moment from her life with you.

Section F

FINAL THOUGHTS

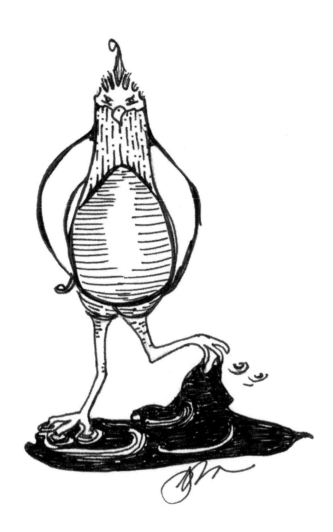

Do you feel stuck?

HOW ALL OF THESE PRACTICES RELATE TO GESTALT THERAPY

"The impasse.... is a natural process that most of us know about, whether we experience it as being stuck in polarizing forces within, or when creating a work of art, writing, composing, and solving problems."
– Lu Grey, Director of BAGI, Bay Area Gestalt Institute

As I said in the beginning these practices, many of which came from Fritz Perls during the late 60s, provide a foundation upon which to experience life more fully. They strengthen our connection with ourselves, and as a result with our friends, family, and the world we live in.

Once you begin to experience them, you might get "stuck", or reach an impasse where you might be blocking yourself from doing them. Ask yourself how you are stopping yourself, and this may lead to many new awarenesses. Often these blocks are beliefs that are getting in your way, or sometimes they might indicate a deeper conflict that needs attending to before going on with the experiments.

You are probably at an *impasse,* as Gestalt folks often say, when some of the following are true for you.

- When you can't stop holding your breath as you talk to someone
- When you are hesitant to go inside yourself to see what you experience
- When you are afraid to look at another without contorting your body in protection
- When you play games to protect yourself with others
- When you constantly hurry and never sit still
- When you are stuck in wanting what you don't have in the moment
- When you don't stop long enough to be in dialogue with others
- When you can't acknowledge what is true for you in the moment
- When you insist on yelling at yourself and calling yourself names
- And when you do the same to others
- When you run away from deep feelings

- And try to live by rationality or 'spirituality' alone
- When you refuse to be aware and curious for fear of having to change
- And when you insist on not even *considering* giving up some of your beliefs
- Or when you can't "be open to the unexpected" without feeling very afraid.

All of the above could be reasons to seek help from a Gestalt group or therapist. And of course in addition to all of these, most people come into therapy when they have problems in one or more of the following areas, which pretty much covers all of our existence! These areas are:

- Health
- Relationships and family
- Money
- Work and career
- Spirituality
- Unfinished business: all of the issues in the recent past as well as the long ago past which haunt us whenever they get a chance.

Acknowledging to ourselves our stuck places is the first step towards healing ourselves.

EXPERIMENT

1. *Make a list of aspects and areas in your life where you feel stuck or at a impasse. Consciously acknowledge these aspects.*

2. *Ask yourself if you wish to explore any of these by yourself, with a friend, through a spiritual practice, or with professional help.*

Whether you are stuck or not, you may wish to find out about Gestalt workshops and other programs in your area. The Gestalt Directory at www.gestalt.org is a great resource with a once-a-month listing of all current programs worldwide.

If you wish to find someone to work with individually who has a background in Gestalt work, you can check the yellow pages of your phone book under psychotherapists, counselors, social workers and psychologists as well as Gestalt centers and institutes.

I purposely did not write this book just about Gestalt *therapy*, as there is a lot written now which focuses primarily on the therapy. Check the internet for other books and material on the subject.

If you are interested in my doing a Gestalt presentation or workshop in your area, or for programs I'm doing in the Pacific Northwest, please visit my website www.cyndysheldon.com.

I wonder where my feet are taking me now?

AFTERWORD

As most of us know, nothing is really fixed in the universe, even when it comes to writing. How does one ever find a place to stop when everything is constantly in motion, and changing from moment to moment? So all I can say is I'm only stopping for the moment. And since this work never ends you or others may carry it on…

EXPERIMENT: THE LAST DANCE

1. *Close your eyes; take a deep breath and allow the themes and experiences you had working with this book to emerge into your awareness. Write them down.*

2. *Go through the table of contents again and see which themes did NOT attract your attention. Is it possible that some of these fall into the category of "But I don't want to be more aware…"?*

Now, may you allow this way of life to unfold for you by listening to your inner self, interacting with your world from moment to moment, and being open to the unexpected. In this way you will become more aware of where your feet are taking you now. Enjoy your journey!

ACKNOWLEDGEMENTS

My first acknowledgements are to the founders of Gestalt Therapy, Fritz & Lore Perls for developing this magnificent work, which has spread and continues to spread world wide. In 1961 I worked with Eugene Sagen and Paul Baum in Berkeley, who were among the few early Gestalt therapists on the West Coast of the US. Then I met and worked with Jim Simkin, who was Fritz' co-leader in many of the workshops in California. I am grateful to all of them for the incredible experiences I've had learning from them.

And then I want to thank all of my colleagues at the Gestalt Institute of San Francisco, particularly Janie Rhyne, Jack Downing, Celia Thompson Taupin, Abe Levitsky, Joe Camhi, Lois Brien, Frank Rubenfeld, Elaine Kepner, Jerry Kogan, John Smolowe, Alyssa Hall, Suzanne Slyman, Lu Grey, and Joan Sullivan. For 25 years we taught together, laughed together, cried together, and sometimes even fought together, just like any close family. And that it was.

All of the clients and students I worked with over these many years gave me an opportunity to develop my way of working with Gestalt, which has led to my elucidating the practices and principles here that I've found to be so useful to my growth and development and theirs as well.

I am very grateful to those on the Navajo Reservation who helped me understand their way of life which has some clear similarities to what I now call the Gestalt way of life. Although I met and worked with many at the Winslow Indian Healthcare Center I am particularly indebted to Isabel Walker, Jones Benally, Vida Khow, Sally Pete, and Frank Armao who taught me a lot about the Navajo world. Ten years with them made a huge impact on me.

The Writer's Conference of the Association for the Advancement of Gestalt Therapy gave me my first boost of support 2 years ago when we met in Pacific Grove California. Specifically thank you to Lu Grey, Liv Estrup, Raissa Veronique, Isabel Frederickson and Joe Hanlon who reviewed my first chapters and gave me a gentle nudge to keep going.

And since then I've been blessed with help from two dear childhood friends, who've read my manuscript and offered helpful feedback and editing skills. Thank you to Erich Schimps, who taught me some of these principles long before I knew anything about Gestalt Therapy, and to Bettina French Pietri, who spent many hours patiently editing these pages.

Sue Drury, a friend from Phoenix, has had extensive Gestalt training and is a professor of psychology. She read the manuscript for content and organization.

And Angela Anderson whom I recently found in Bellingham, did the delightful illustrations for this book.

If it weren't for all of you, this book could never have been written. I thank you from the bottom of my heart.

ABOUT THE AUTHOR

CYNDY SHELDON, MSW, BCD, who studied with Gestalt founder Fritz Perls MD, PhD, was one of the organizers of the original Gestalt Institute of San Francisco in 1967 where she taught for 25 years, as well as in Europe when Gestalt therapy first began appearing there.

Inspired to follow her bliss in search of a more spiritual orientation, she moved to Sedona, Arizona for a few years, the metaphysical Mecca of the USA. Here she began discovering similarities between some Buddhist teachings, the work of Eckhart Tolle and Gestalt. When she discovered the nearby Navajo Reservation, she connected deeply with the elders and the medicine people at a part-time job with a Navajo health clinic. There she learned of similarities in the Navajo way of life and Gestalt's timeless understandings.

Guided to move back to the West Coast, this time to the State of Washington, she began experiencing a renaissance of interest in Gestalt practices and therapy. As a result she and colleagues began co-creating a Gestalt community in the Pacific Northwest, which is growing. For the last few years she has been teaching Gestalt in workshops and on-going training classes in both Bellingham, Washington (where she lives) and in the Seattle area. This, her first book, is doing very well with her colleagues, trainees and those who know very little about Gestalt.

Now in her 78th year, she is integrating the many experiences she's had with the Gestalt founders, the metaphysical and spiritual time in Arizona and among the Navajo, and is eager to share them with all who are curious and interested.

ABOUT THE ARTIST

ANGELA ANDERSON is an art educator and freelance artist in Bellingham, Washington. She has worked across several media, including painting, collage, assemblage and drawing. Frequently she gravitates towards bird and fish imagery in her work. This is her first book illustration project.

78011708R00075

Made in the USA
San Bernardino, CA
31 May 2018